The Biggest City You've Never Heard Of

A story of personal growth through the challenges of life in modern day China

Dr Andy Wynn

(Foreword by Andy & Julie Wynn)

ISBN: 978-1-0818-6703-4

This book is dedicated to our daughter, Heather.
Julie and I are immensely proud of the new life you have made for
yourself in China.

CONTENTS

PREFACE

If you've ever fancied a nibble on a Nuclear Frog, if you've ever wanted to experience the 'delicious fun of killing fish in the rain', if you've ever wondered what's it's like to take a dump balancing precariously on two thin concrete posts with your backside hanging out over a cliff, then this is the book for you.

We are Andy & Julie Wynn, and we had the privilege of living in China for over 6 years. Our experience was both funny and shocking in equal measures, but never dull. Our story is eye opening and informative, and unlocks the real China, what life is really like on the streets in modern Asia. Often challenging and uncomfortable, certainly educational, but definitely a lot of fun. China forces you to question everything you've ever known, everything you were taught, everything you think is right about how to do even the most mundane of everyday things.

If you want to know what life is like living on the 'Eye of the Cock of China', then this is essential and entertaining reading.

DR ANDY WYNN

FOREWORD

We are not back-packing hippy types, out to travel the backwaters and nether regions of China on a shoe string, eating extreme street food and trying to get in touch with our Chinese zodiac sign. We are not explorers seeking to paddle the enormous length of the Yangtze to its source and then trek the little known uninhabitable regions of the Tibetan Himalayas, living off tree bark and slugs. We are not adventurers, but we are on an adventure. We are normal, professional people, sent out from our home in the UK to do a job. But sent to a place that at times is so unrecognisable and incongruent to us, that it might as well be an alien planet.

We are Andy & Julie Wynn, and what we learnt in our 6 years living in China, is that the China expat experience is truly beneficial for both mind and body; it expands your knowledge and appreciation of the world, it helps you become more tolerant of different peoples and cultures, and it improves your thighs no end with all that squatting for the toilet.

We are not pioneers or trail blazers. There have been business people and tourists travelling out to China for decades, and in some cases much longer. We don't pretend we have done something unique. There is a thriving expat community in every city in China and Asia. But what we have done still takes guts and is not for everyone. What we do know, is that everyone's expat experience is a one off, and we have our own story to tell. Often challenging and uncomfortable, certainly educational, but definitely a lot of fun. China forces you to question everything you've ever known, everything you were taught, everything you think is right about how to do even the most mundane of everyday stuff. Despite what you hear on the news about the economy over there, China is still the new Wild West, and remains a real land of opportunity.

But the expat experience can make you or break you, it can enrich your life and relationships or it can destroy your marriage. We have seen guys use the expat life to get away from their wives, and leave them back in their home country for 2 or 3 years. That is never going to help a relationship. These guys usually end up getting a local girlfriend and basically leading two lives. Others probably had the best of intentions when moving to take a new post in China; a great career move, more money, better prospects. But 2 or 3 years living on your own, half way around the planet from your spouse and family, is always tougher than you think it is going to be. Loneliness will wear you down, and even the toughest of men will seek companionship eventually. We have seen it happen. The other type that moves to China for an expat posting is the one that doesn't give a shit. They may take their spouse with them. But they are out to have a good time wherever and with whomever they wish. So even though their wife may be sitting at home in their apartment in China, they still build a double life for themselves around the less wholesome hot spots of the city. We have seen all of these types. There are also the young families that get posted to China. We were always in admiration for those couple's that take young kids with them, very hard work when you have a whole new world to cope with.

We were two of the lucky few. We went out to China for 3 years and ended up staying for over 6. And that is not an uncommon story. Those that make it there often learn to love it and often get the chance to extend their contracts or change jobs to extend their stay, or even end up living there permanently.

Whilst there is plenty in our book that we hope is amusing and pokes fun at some of the things we have seen and experienced, this book is in no way intended to take the mickey out of the Chinese people. Rather it is meant to highlight the crazy stuff that emerges from a clash of cultures and incongruent ways of doing things. Our 6 years was an eye opening experience that held up a mirror to ourselves. It is easy to think that the way you go about your daily lives is 'normality' and the way you were brought up to do things is the 'right' way. But it is amazing to discover how different cultures view what is normal and how they have built up a completely different set of rules for their daily routine. What we learnt in Asia is that there are not necessarily right or wrong ways of doing things, but there are certainly different approaches to getting through the grind of daily life. This challenged constantly our perception of what is the right way to do things, and ultimately changed the way we behave and the way we view life. You have to learn from your experience or what's the point?

What we do want to stress is that everything described in this book is true, everything we saw and experienced was real. We have not made any of it up, though we have declined to name names to protect the innocent and avoid embarrassment (often our own). For the sake of building a narrative to weave our experiences around, this book is written from Andy's perspective, but tells the story of both of our experiences, occasionally separate, often shared, always entertaining.

We certainly feel tremendously enriched and positively changed by our time in China, not least because of all the great friendships we built. Some of our closest and dearest friends are either still there or have dissipated back to their home countries or on to new expat assignments in new locations. And that is an additional benefit of expat life, not only do you gain from all the experiences of your host country, you also gain from crossing paths with so many other nationalities that are going through the same experience as you. We moved to a 'smaller' city in China, and so the friends we made were not just a bunch of other British people on assignment. If we had ended up in the metropolises of Shanghai or Beijing, that is often the experience expats have, they end up hanging out with their own kind. But in our small Chinese city, there were very few British people, very few of any non-Chinese communities, so our experience was truly international. Our circle of friends were from Spain, Norway, Brazil, Columbia, Korea, Japan, Malaysia, China, Philippines, France, Germany, Finland, Sweden, Australia, USA, and many other countries. This above all broadened our life experience during our time in China, and truly turned us into global citizens.

When we first told friends, family and colleagues we were moving to China, the usual response was shock. 'Why do you want to go there?' they would say in mild disgust. Over time we discovered that many people back home still had a very old fashioned attitude to China and still thought of China as a backward country. Even our daughter, who eventually followed us out to live and work in China a couple of years later, said that before she went to Shanghai, she thought the streets would be filled with rickshaws pulled by peasants in coolie hats. Andy had been travelling to China on business for several years, so he knew the reality was anything but what everyone was saying, but still, it amazed us that people still thought like this given all the media coverage of China. Even after we moved out to China, whenever we returned to England, people's usual attitude to us was of mild pity. They seemed to think that we lived a meagre lifestyle in difficult circumstances, without all the comforts of home. The reality, as you will read, could not be further from the truth. And once any of these people actually came out to visit us, their mind was blown away by what they saw and their attitude became completely transformed. 'Now I understand why you like living here', one of Andy's colleagues finally admitted to him after his visit.

So we were motivated to write this book to help educate people in the West and work to dispel these misinformed attitudes that many still have about China. We hope you have a chuckle or two along the way at the absurdity that arises from the clash of cultures, and take some time to reflect on the how's and the why's as you're tackling your everyday life.

And if you are ever lucky enough to have the opportunity to visit China, whether for business or pleasure, we hope our book helps you in making better informed decisions so that you can enjoy the experience much more. And if you ever have the chance to live and work there, then our advice is take it, you will not regret it.

We hope you enjoy our story.

Andy & Julie Wynn

DR ANDY WYNN

CHAPTER 1

THE EYE ON THE COCK OF CHINA (OR MOVING TO DALIAN AND OUR FIRST STEPS)

'The Biggest City You've Never Heard Of', that's what I learnt to reply to people around the world when they asked where we lived in China. Dalian is just a small tier 2 city of nearly 7 million people. That always blows people's minds in the West. It is located in Liaoning province, in the North East of China, around 3 hours' drive from the North Korean border. It's not even the capital of its province, that's Shenyang. China is on a vast scale, and it's hard to adjust your perspective to it. The cities are big and numerous, the population is vast, the buildings and infrastructure are immense. China is a country of mind blowing facts. There are more than 100 cities in China with a population over 1 million people. The population of

Beijing is the same as the whole of Australia. There are over 1.3 billion people living in China today, that's a billion more than in the US. To put it another way, one in five people on planet Earth today are Chinese. And we were heading there to live.

I had been offered a job to go and work in China, to build a new factory for my company, on a three year contract. A big decision for anyone, in many ways, both exciting and scary at the same time. It was a tremendous challenge both career-wise and lifestyle-wise. I had been travelling to China on business several times over the previous few years, so I was familiar enough with many aspects of just being there, though I was certainly not naïve enough to think that living there would not be a very different kettle of sea cucumbers. Julie on the other hand had never been to Asia and only knew it through my tales of the insane drinking culture and challenging toilet experiences that I had encountered on my business trips. Not a good start to selling it to her. Despite the scariness of the whole 'diving into the unknown', it was something I really wanted to do. I had always loved Asia and China in particular, and I had always wanted some overseas work experience to put on my CV. I was also of an age and with sufficient wisdom by then that I understood that you have to grab opportunities with both hands and jump straight in if you want to develop as a person and make the most of your life and that you inevitably will make a few mistakes along the way on your journey. I knew that life in China would not be easy in plenty of ways, but I also knew that it would be an experience that would enrich our lives in ways that we could not yet know. And also, it's only three years, it's not for the rest of your life, so why not? Julie being the wonderful supportive wife that she is agreed to give it a go.

A good friend of ours said something profound to us

recently, 'we each have two lives, and the second one begins when you realise that you have only one.' In hindsight, I can see how true this is, and our second life definitely started when we made that decision to move to China, because it immediately began to change our whole outlook on life, and on what is important to us.

There is no better example of this than when starting our preparations to leave the UK. Our 'second life' attitude kicked in right from the outset. Up to that point I had followed a pretty normal life path; get an education, get a job, build a career, get a wife, get a house, raise a family, get a divorce, get slammed for child support payments, etc. Fortunately Julie saved me from all this, but that's another story. But the main point of all this is that it was the typical hedonistic approach to life, buying a house, buying a car, buying TVs, buying things, things, things and accumulating 'stuff'. When you realise you are going to move across the planet to live in a foreign country, what do you do with all this 'stuff'? Do you take it with you? It really challenges your attachment to all your 'stuff' and previously, in my 'first life', I was very attached to my 'stuff', after all, I had worked very hard to buy it all. Now, in this 'second life' that I had started, I realised that actually, it was more important to me to go and live in China and enjoy a full Chinese experience with Julie, and that remaining attached to all my 'stuff' would just keep pulling us back to our old life. I realised that 'experiences' are more important than 'things'. So very quickly I understood that I did not want to take any of our old 'stuff' with us, and that we were just going to move with a few suitcases with the essentials of life, clothes and shoes and a few basics to get us started. Apart from that, I knew that we would not be taking any of our furniture or TVs, and that I would need to look for a fully furnished apartment in Dalian, though at that early stage we didn't have an apartment arranged. So what to do with all your 'stuff'? Do you put it in storage? Many people in our situation do and the company will usually cover the cost. But I figured why put a TV into storage for 3 years, maybe more? By the time we get back it will be old technology and just become junk. All the expat friends we subsequently met in China and across Asia all had the same decisions to make. Some chose to take all their furniture with them and have it shipped over by the company. These were usually the ones with nice expensive antique furniture. But for me, this just made your new apartment in China a little version of your home back in the old country. That was definitely not what I wanted. I came to realise that part of the fun of being an expat is just starting over again in new surroundings, surrounded by 'new stuff'. So I found moving to China a very therapeutic experience. It helped me cut my hedonistic ties with my possessions. I gave away so much stuff to friends, family and charity shops, I sold a few things, and I threw away lots of things as junk. All to de-clutter our life, so that we could start afresh our new life in China. Three years was a long way in the future, and I knew that we could not predict that far ahead what our life would be like, where we would be and what we would be doing. As it turned out it was all a very smart decision, as we ended up staying in China for over 6 years. By then, my huge wide-screen Cathode Ray Tube TV that weighed 100 lbs would definitely have been a museum piece by the time we came back if I'd put it into storage.

Once we had made our decision on the big move, we started doing our homework on the internet, to try to understand better what we had let ourselves in for, to start looking for apartments, and to make some plans for what we might be doing in and around the Dalian area at the weekends. When all you are restricted to is English language websites it is very limiting. I'm sure Chinese language websites have lots of great detailed information, but at that stage, our Chinese language skills were non-existent, and so as an English speaker it was a bit tough in 2011 finding out good information on the city and certainly very difficult trying to look for apartments. My company was going to help us out with the latter of course, but we were just eager to get started. One good website we did find was the local Dalian government English language official tourist website, which had a lot of great information and showed off many wonderful places we might visit in our free time. It made it look a very exciting and interesting place, much more so than our own home town in the UK. The website was all written in awkward pigeon English, which made for some interesting phraseology and a taste of things to come in terms of our future Chinglish experiences. The opening page was particularly memorable. In describing Dalian's location, it made reference to the fact that mainland China is shaped like a chicken or a rooster, and so the official English Language tourist strapline proudly announced that Dalian is the 'Eye on the Cock of China', that certainly sold it for me!

Soon after agreeing to the move, we flew over to China for some orientation time, to make sure Julie would be comfortable with the whole thing before I signed a new employment contract and fully committed. I was eager to sell the whole China experience to Julie of course, so I had booked business class seats all the way and we were booked into the luxurious Kempinksi hotel, that I had stayed at already a few times on previous business trips, a modern hotel with a great location opposite Labour Park in the centre of the city. We flew the 12 hours from Europe to Beijing (the longest flight Julie had ever done) and guess what, a massive storm hit and we got grounded in Beijing.

Our flight was cancelled, with hundreds of others, and we were all bussed off to some very basic hotel, a long way out on the outskirts of the city, for an uncomfortable night's sleep. Not the great, luxurious start to Julie's Chinese experience that I had planned. Instead, her first taste of China was of the chaos, confusion and headless chicken behaviour that the Chinese display so well in such situations.

We finally arrived in Dalian the next day and the week could start properly, with a mixture of work, dinners with colleagues, some free time around the city and starting to look for apartments. It seemed a strange but exciting place. Even though it was not my first time there, I was looking at everything with very different eyes, knowing that we were actually going to be moving there to live. I scrutinised everything with an intensity that I hadn't before as just a passing visitor, analysing everything we saw, looking under the hood, as we walked down the street. The number one thing on your mind once you've made the decision to move is, where are you going to live? So we started scouting about a soon as we could. Lots of decisions to be made here. Do you want to go native for the full on local experience? Or do you want the more cosy cotton wool experience of Western style living? Leaving Julie at home whilst I went to work every day, plus travelling away for weeks at a time on business trips, weighed heavily on my mind, so it was always my intention to find a serviced apartment for us, so she would have immediate support to fall back on. The problem was that as a tier 2 city, Dalian was not as developed as Shanghai or Beijing in this respect and there were not many serviced apartments to choose from. We visited a handful of places, but it was usually like going back to my student digs, very basic accommodation with cheap, scratched furniture. There were some nice big villas on the coast to rent but Julie would be very lonely there. So it was not easy to find somewhere that I would be happy to leave Julie on her own, it was clearly going to take some time and effort before we found the right place. So our week was up and it was back to the UK to continue our preparations for the move. There was no great rush, we had a few weeks to organise ourselves and it was pretty likely that I would go back out to Dalian to set things up before Julie followed, so there was always likely to be a transition period. When I moved to Dalian officially in October, as we had no apartment fixed up, I had to stay in a hotel for many weeks while I did my work and continued to view apartments. I lived in the Intercontinental hotel for several weeks, in a business class room, living out of a couple of suitcases. I had my breakfast and dinner every evening in their business lounge on the top floor of the hotel. I enjoyed great views of the city every evening as I looked out wondering, where are we going to end up living? It was a weird, a little lonely, but an exciting time, as I knew change was coming. My perseverance in apartment viewings finally paid off when I found the Shangri-La Residences. Imagine my delight when I found out that the number one five star hotel in the city also had a separate apartment block of serviced apartments, especially for expats. Pricey of course, but it turned out to be a life enhancing decision to move there.

There were so many adjustments we needed to make to settle into our new life, even at the most basic level. This was the first time we had ever lived in an apartment in a city centre. Before that we had always lived in a house with a garden. I managed to get an apartment on the 28th floor, right at the top of the building, so we could be away from the constant traffic noise down on the street. This place was situated on the busiest street in the city, in the heart of the Financial District, so it was non-stop day and night. Great fun if you like a full on life, but not so good if you value the occasional night's sleep. The Shangri-La was an amazing place to start out life in a strange and foreign land. All the comforts of a 5 star hotel, with real down and dirty street life right across the street. The best of both worlds. We lived there for over 6 years, and over that time we lived through many changes to the hotel, to the residences and across the city. We saw many restaurants come and go, saw the city grow and modernise at a rapid pace and best of all, we met some amazing people along the way and made many wonderful friends, all thanks to the Shangri-La. We still feel lucky every day that we settled down there and made it our home for so long. It helped us enormously to acclimatise to our new situation and gave me the peace of mind that I could get on with my job every day whilst Julie was nice and cosy and safe.

The Shangri-La Residences was a high rise apartment building attached to the main hotel. So being a resident there gave you access to all the benefits of the hotel, all the restaurants, the gym, the swimming pool, tennis courts, plus the residences had a dedicated support staff of wonderfully friendly and helpful people. Of course, this all came at a price, it was five stars after all, but it was so worth it. Being able to go to a five star gym every day without even leaving the building was an amazing privilege that I still value to this day, and was a big decision factor in our next move after China, but that's another story. Our closest restaurant was the Nishimura, one of the top Japanese restaurants in the city, which we visited twice a week, every week, for the most amazing sushi and sashimi, and again we didn't even have to step outside the building to enjoy it. Talk about convenience.

The first year we lived there, we would regularly go to

the supermarket to buy groceries and cook frequently at home, just as we would have back in the UK. But over time, we came to realise that the price of the kinds of things as Westerners that we like to buy in the supermarkets was quite expensive, and the price of eating out was relatively low and much better quality than we could produce at home. So after the first year, we went less and less often to the supermarket for groceries and started eating out at restaurants more and more often, to the point that in the last three years, it was very rare that we ever cooked at home, particularly as we had access to the hotel room service menu on the other end of the phone or home delivery through numerous smartphone apps. There was one funny incident in our 4th year at the Shangri-La, after they had done a major renovation of all the apartments. Our apartment had been fully refitted and modernised, everything was brand new. The kitchen was brand new. After several months, I remember one of Julie's friends coming round and she commented on the kitchen, 'how do you keep your cooker so clean?' I had to have a good laugh at that, 'pretty easy when your never use it', I thought!

In fact, I came to learn that the food lifestyle we had fallen into is pretty common in China. Later on, when I was placing my own overseas employees in China on short term contracts, and we were searching for accommodation for them in the major cities, I discovered that there are so many cheap local eateries on the street that it is not uncommon for an apartment in a big city, certainly for a small studio flat, not to have a kitchen, because people are expected to eat out on the street. You can get a great bowl of noodles for 10 RMB, so it's really cheap. The only problem I faced with this was when I was placing one guy in Shanghai and he told me he was a vegetarian. Not much in the way of vegetarian restaurants on the average street of

Shanghai, even the stir fried vegetable dishes have bacon in them to add flavour, so we had to upgrade him so he could have a kitchen and look after himself.

Life on the streets in China took some getting used to. One of the first things that strikes you is that snorting, gobbing and spitting seem to be national pastimes. No one who visits China can fail to be confronted by, and get grossed out by, this behaviour within an hour of arriving. When my daughter followed me out to China and moved to Shanghai, this was one of the reasons she cited for wanting to return home after the first year. Usually a particular favourite of middle aged, seemingly unsophisticated males in China, there seems to be a competition on the street for who can snort the loudest and longest, who can roll the biggest, stickiest gob ball around their mouth and who can launch it out onto the most inappropriate public surface. I've seen it all, mega-spitting walking along the street, gungy greebos launched in shopping malls, succulent sputum dropped onto airport departure halls, and coughed up conkers left in five star hotel lobbies. Really nowhere is out of bounds for these guys, there is no sanctuary from their pursuit.

It gets to the point that you have to be ever watchful walking down the street, and finding yourself having to weave your way down the sidewalk to avoid all the gob patches. While middle aged men in China love their spitting, the middle aged ladies love their little dogs, and so they also leave their own special mark on the sidewalk. So walking down the average city street can turn out to be an assault course of sidestepping sputum and dodging dog turds.

And you will never get used to all the spitting and hawking. Even at the dinner table, people can enjoy an impromptu quick snort and swallow of their phlegm. At least I haven't yet see anyone spit theirs out onto the table, but I guess it's only a matter of time. The whole 'noises around the dinner table' thing is also very off putting for us Westerners, who have been brought up with a whole different set of table manners. Across much of Asia, not just China, making loud slurping noises when eating your food and belching afterwards are all considered compliments to the chef about how tasty their food is. There is a kind of logic to this, but it absolutely goes against everything I was ever taught by my parents at the dinner table, don't slurp your food, don't burp, and certainly don't fart. It is pretty weird to sit next to one of your Chinese colleagues for lunch, someone who you know is a well-educated and well-travelled modern professional person, and listen to them slurp as they suck up their noodles. It just seems so wrong, it's so unexpected and the noise really grates inside you. I have seen some of my Western colleagues try to make the effort and join in with the slurping, good for them, well intentioned, but it just doesn't fit with them and somehow the noise they make and the technique they use just isn't quite right. It's like seeing a white man with dreadlocks.

And when you're out on the street and in restaurants, another thing that is difficult to get used to again is all the smoking. I grew up during the whole transition in the West from a society where smoking was acceptable and commonplace, to gradually see it stigmatised, clamped down on by health campaigns and slowly driven out by legislation, to the point that it is rare to see smokers now and never in restaurants. And in hindsight, with respect to public spaces, it all seems so logical. What was all that business in the past with having a smoking section on an airplane? How was that ever going to work? It just seems so silly now. But when you move to China, you have to step back in time through the smoke screen by 30 years, to relive those experiences of your childhood. Though thankfully they don't have a smoking section on Chinese aircraft. Walking down a street in China you will see a lot of people smoking, usually men. Maybe it helps to fuel their snorting and spitting compulsion. Even in shops and shopping malls they will be smoking. But the worst is in restaurants, when you're trying to eat your dinner, that is the most off-putting. But it is not exactly the same as 30 years ago in the West. China has health campaigns and public information on the dangers of smoking and they have laws banning smoking in public spaces in the big cities, but people just ignore them. A big challenge is that cigarettes are just too cheap. Chinese brands can cost as little as 10 RMB for a packet, though just like with alcohol, there are also fake cigarettes, though how anyone can smoke these things packed with chemicals is well beyond me. So given there is health education and laws banning smoking in public places, why do so many Chinese still smoke? China is the number one producer of tobacco in the world, and the number one consumer with 350 million Chinese smokers. Yet this trade is controlled by one single state-owned company and generates up to 10% of the annual government's tax revenue. Tough income for the government to give up. An even more difficult fact to swallow is that almost 60% of male Chinese doctors are still smokers, what message does that give out to the masses?

You will also inevitably encounter from time to time during your life in China, some occasional racism and xenophobia. I guess this goes for any foreigner in any country, but it's going to be most obvious when you look, dress and act so differently from the locals, and in China, there is no hiding that you are from out of town. At its most mild and common it is no more than people stopping and staring at you in the street. This is more common the further away you get from the big cities. Obviously in Shanghai and Beijing, the local population are used to seeing Westerners on the streets every day, so they don't generally turn a hair when you walk past. But in other cities, and certainly out in rural areas, you can get stared at much more routinely because you are a rare site for some of these people. This was particularly true in Dalian, not so much with the local people, but more due to the fact that Dalian is a vacation place for the region, so you get large groups of 'farmers' travelling from the less developed parts of the country to Dalian for their family holiday. Some of these people act like they have never seen a Westerner in their life before, and some of them probably haven't. They will stop and stare open mouthed at you, the kids will tug on their mothers sleeve and point at you shouting 'wàiguórén, wàiguórén' (foreigner). And inevitably some will want to have their photo taken with you. The other word for foreigner that you will regularly hear shouted at you in the street or whispered behind your back in shops, while people nudge each other and point, is 'lǎowài'. 'Wàiguórén' is the more formal, correct word for foreigner, whilst 'lǎowài' is more of a slang term, though usually used in a neutral context, it can sometimes be used in an impolite sense in some circumstances, a little like being called 'gringo' in Mexico.

It is part of the charm of being a stranger in a strange land that you become part of the tourist experience for these people. Maybe it's their first time to a big city, so maybe it's their first time seeing a foreigner in the flesh. Quite something for them I imagine. Every time Julie and I took an afternoon trip out to Xinghǎi Square or Binhǎi Lù (the coast road), we would get stopped so families could have their picture taken with us. It's no different for us I guess when we travel to new and exotic places for our vacations. Part of the memories you bring back are those photos you get standing with a group of pretty girls in grass skirts in Hawaii, or with flamenco dancers in Seville, or with guys dressed as roman soldiers and gladiators outside the Coliseum in Rome (those guys are so aggressive). The difference of course is that these people are only dressed up like that for you the tourist and expect some money from you for the privilege of taking the photo with them. In Dalian we got nothing. Our record one afternoon was that we were stopped and had to pose for photos 'twelve times' in about 3 hours. At that point I started to think we should start charging for our services. 10 RMB a pop could have been a nice little side earner for us. I know some of my friends got a bit fed up with it, especially those who were pushing kids around in a pushchair, as ageing Chinese ladies always wanted to stop them and take a photo with their kids, so I can understand their concern. But Julie and I did not have that problem and really we didn't mind stopping and having a chat with these strangers. It was a great part of us mingling with real Chinese, and a great way to practice our language skills. Over the years, as we got better at speaking Chinese, we could have some really pleasant simple chats with these Dalian vacationers, and of course they thought it was great that their 'wàiguórén' could speak some Chinese.

At the other end of the xenophobia spectrum, there is a much more menacing side to your China experience. As a foreigner you will be targeted for scams and threats, especially in the big cities. Inevitably some rogues think you are just an ignorant tourist, flush with money, and ripe for the picking. It starts as soon as you land at the airport and step out of arrivals. All the dodgy black cab drivers are always waiting for you to drag you off to their unlicensed taxi for an extortionate risky car journey to drop you somewhere not quite outside your hotel. In Shanghai's People's Square you will be targeted by pretty young ladies who speak excellent English and offer to take you to a tea ceremony where you will be charge overinflated prices for your beverage. Late at night you will have a guy run in and steal your taxi at the last second outside a night club to try to get you to start a fight so he can call his policeman friend to force you to pay a cash fine. Like in any big city around the world, you need to have your wits about you when travelling. I regularly experienced all of these and many more, every more creative ways of trying to part you from your cash. You just need to develop a thick skin and brush these people off. If something doesn't feel right, it isn't.

You will also be hounded by beggars in the big cities and around tourist spots. Some are genuinely needy, but many are part of organised gangs, some even displaying fake disabilities to grab your sympathy. I remember one particularly persistent guy in Guangzhou who was begging at the side of the street by a row of shops. He had no legs and 'walked' around using wooden blocks in his hands. For whatever reason he targeted me as I walked down the street. I discovered his wooden blocks also had a secondary use, as they were great for banging his targets on the ankle to coerce them into handing over some money. When I ignored him, he started chasing me down the street about 100m on his wooden blocks. He was pretty fast on those things, and I had to break into a trot to finally ditch him. The whole thing did feel pretty comical to me, despite the tragedy of his situation, and I couldn't help giggling as he was pursuing me down the street. This probably didn't help and may have spurred him on. There was another guy close to our home in Dalian that we used to pass most days when we walked down the main street. He was in a bad way, the sort of things that you could not fake. Poor guy. He could not have got to his position in the main street without help, so must have been dropped off every morning. He was a charming guy with a great smile, and used to grin from ear to ear whenever he saw Julie walking down the street. We would always stop and give him something. I used to give him all the bags of change that I would regularly accumulate. I liked to think it was a mutually beneficial relationship. He was only there one season and we never saw him again in subsequent years.

One of the deals you often have when your company sends you on assignment in China is they give you a driver. Why? Well partly that's the culture in Asian businesses, the senior guys get driven around. This would be much too expensive an extravagance in the West, but in China it is affordable. But the main reason is that if you drive yourself (and it is possible for you to get a driving license in China), then as a Westerner behind a wheel you tend to stick out when sitting in traffic. And the risk is that you become an insurance target for every wide boy looking to make a fast buck by driving into you and claiming off your insurance. The Chinese driving style tend to be notoriously dangerous as well. So it doubles the risk. Even as a pedestrian, the road can be a very dangerous place.

Why did the expat cross the road? Because he was playing chicken. Crossing the road in the middle of a Chinese city is a big scary challenge. There are usually multiple lanes, all filled with cars driving at a crazy pace, 30% of them taxis. When you first arrive in China, standing at the side of the road, gazing out at the rows and rows of vehicles thundering past, is a frightening place to be. Timing your first step into such a hostile environment can be a life changing decision. Once behind the wheel, Chinese guys take no prisoners. On the roads in China, size is everything and the biggest thing driving down the road rules the road, and you are definitely not the biggest thing in the road when you step out. That's why the Chinese have developed a technique for crossing the road. They gather into a large group at the side and then start to cross, and suddenly the mob of people spilling out onto the road becomes the biggest thing in the road, and everything will stop for you. Logical really.

If you do choose to drive, and I only remember one of my friends that chose to do this during his time in Dalian, then you will have the Chinese traffic to deal with, and that is yet another thing that is difficult to get used to for foreigners. You will see all the dubious and dangerous driving behaviours that have been slowly stamped out now on Western roads; tailgating, undertaking, weaving between lanes, driving on the hard shoulder down the highway, using smartphones whilst driving and generally aggressive driving. You have to be on high alert constantly when driving in China. The mechanics of driving around China is all based around the US system, so they drive on the left and can turn right on a red light if the coast is clear of pedestrians. But being China, they interpret this rule as meaning that they can turn right whatever. If you are crossing the road and your green man gives you right of way, do not assume the cars will stop for you. Those turning right against a red light, will come at you, they will not stop, be warned. You will have many close calls with cars as you try to circumnavigate the road system as a pedestrian. Red lights are just considered optional in China, and the rules of the road favour the car not you. There will be times when you feel like banging on the hood of a car as it screeches to a halt an inch from your knees. I have seen friends do this, but all this accomplishes is an angry driver screaming in your face and a gathering crowd of Chinese onlookers, all with their phones out videoing you, waiting for the punch up. The best technique I developed for crossing the road, if there isn't a crowd of Chinese to join in with, requires a lot of confidence and experience with Chinese roads. If I want to cross the road I step out to the edge of the first lane and walk towards the oncoming cars, it is much easier to judge how fast they are coming if you are moving towards them, and can more easily and safely judge the gap and pass to the edge of the next lane. You will also hear a lot of car horns being used in China. In the UK, drivers only use the horn as an aggressive 'f**k you' signal to another road user, but in China it is used much more as it was intended, as a means to flag up to other road users that the vehicle is there and to take care. But the result is that streets can become really loud with car horns blaring out all the time.

But it's not always the cars you need to worry about as a pedestrian. Motorcycles and bicycles rarely stop at red lights and often don't even slow down. They also have a habit of being driven the wrong way down streets, against the flow of traffic and down the sidewalk. The most dangerous are the electric motorcycles, because they are completely silent. You just can't hear them coming as you walk down the street. Too often I have had these electric motorbikes whizz past inches from me at high speed. Given the chaos on the streets, foreigners often say to me that they wonder why they don't see more accidents. But my experience of driving to and from the office every day was that I saw an accident or major road traffic incident every single day of my 25 minute commute. So given the special challenges of life on the road in China, overall, its best to take the driver option, someone who knows the local driving style.

The risks are considerable. More than 700 people are killed on Chinese roads every day, that's over a quarter of a million people every year, of which, over half are pedestrians and cyclists. And road accidents are now the leading cause of death in China for young adults. If you are unlucky enough to get hit by a car crossing the road, beware, a disturbing new trend has been emerging in China where drivers may well reverse back over you to make sure they finish you off rather than leave you injured. Why do drivers do this? Better to have to make a one off compensation payment to the dead person's family than be lumbered with paying compensation to the injured party for the rest of their lives. This type of legislation has meant that passing drivers and pedestrians are also now reluctant to stop and help injured road accident victims for fear they will be accused of causing the accident and held liable for compensation payments. There have been several high profile cases of this in recent years, the most memorable of which was the tragic case of a two-year-old girl who died after she was run over by two separate vehicles, neither of which stopped, and then ignored by 18 passers-by before a road sweeper finally stopped to help her. The Chinese internet is littered with scary, toe curling videos of road accidents like this that make for very difficult viewing. So my message is, stay safe on the roads in China, take no risks.

Since the Chinese economy has grown so tremendously in the last 30 years, like with many other things, China is now the number one car manufacturer in the world. All of the big Western car companies are over there and all have joint ventures with Chinese state owned companies. In the past, a Western company was not allowed to set up its own wholly owned business in China, you had to have a joint venture with a government owned company. Each company had to have a government representative on the pay roll as part of the company management. This has all since changed though and Western companies are now free to set up their own 100% owned company within China. Alongside the Western joint ventures, many indigenous Chinese car manufacturers have emerged and it is now common place to see a wide array of local brands on the road as you're driving around, including, Great Wall, Geely, Dongfeng, Chang'an, Jiangling, and the largest Chinese manufacturer and my favourite name, BYD, which stands for 'Build Your Dreams', what a great name for a car company.

One of the many positive consequences of my time in China, one of the many ways in which the lifestyle has changed me for the better, is that having a personal driver for six years finally weaned me off the old fashioned concept of car ownership. I did not own a car for all of our time in China, and instead had use of a company vehicle. This opened up my eyes to the benefits of not owning a car; no tax and insurance to arrange, no maintenance to do, no arranging for repairs or testing. It just takes a whole chunk of non-value added, wasted time out of your life. Time you can focus on more valuable things. Ever since I have returned to live in Europe, I still do not own a car, preferring to rent or lease cars now. Let someone else have all the hassle of the ownership and maintenance of the car. I grew up in an age and in a society where the aspirations of life included owning you own house and owning one or more cars. I knew no other way but to strive toward these things. My time and circumstances in China have taught me to see things very differently now, and as our society and economy has slowly changed to a more service oriented one, where everything has become a service and almost everything can be hired, it has allowed me to break the cycle of my old fashioned aspirations. I much prefer the freedom of car leasing now.

I was amazed the first time I went to our original company in Dalian around 20 years ago, there were about 50 staff in the offices, but 8 of them were drivers. This seemed an unbelievable waste of money to me. I thought, how do they keep all these guys busy? And the answer of course was that they didn't. Even years later when I moved there permanently to live, there were still 6 drivers, but they all had fancy titles. One guy was the Office Manager, a really loud mouth opinionated guy. I heard plenty of tales about how he spent the afternoons at the local sauna or swimming pool. He was basically the local fixer and had 'connections', so people were afraid of him. That's why no one had the guts to get rid of him. Though he was a good karaoke singer. This was all part of the local culture of doing business in China, this was all normal to them and just another example of how I brought my Western attitudes to their country, resulting in yet another major culture clash for me.

It was a similar deal in our Indian factories as well, with lots of drivers on the staff, though not so extreme as in China. Though thinking back, one of the UK companies I started working at in the early 90s had a kind of a general maintenance guy working there. He told me that he used to be the chauffeur for the directors. This must have been in the 70s/early 80s. He said he wore a peak cap and the whole get up, driving round a fancy Mercedes. He told me tales about the directors dining room that had its own bar, and how they'd all get in there every afternoon for 'meetings' and he'd have to drive everyone home drunk afterwards. And this was every day. I guess this was what they call the 'good old days'? How business has changed. I doubt any of those guys are still alive now, probably died of liver disease long ago. But my point is, whether in UK, China or India, businesses tend to develop along similar lines, they're all just at different points along that same development line. Our company in China today has even fewer drivers, so the downsizing trend is continuing.

But I digress. So we land in China and I am given a driver. Now this presents another new problem for the expat. Most of us are not used to having drivers, or maids (yes, we had one of those as well). It feels like having servants. But we are not used to how to interact with them. The biggest issue from day one for us was how to behave with the driver. Do you sit in the back or in the front with him? Do you treat them as an employee or as a colleague? Are they available 24 hours a day or what? It is pretty weird not being able to jump in your own car and drive wherever you want. There is definitely a loss of freedom you feel, having to call the driver every time. But for short journeys taxis are very cheap and very plentiful in a Chinese city, 10% of what I would pay in Europe. The classic problem with Chinese taxis though is, no seat belts in the back.

I was extremely lucky with our drivers. Because I had been visiting the company a few times prior to moving out there, I had got friendly with one of the drivers that used to pick me up at the airport, Mr Huang. He was a fun guy, always smiling and upbeat. We developed a friendly relationship. Pretty good considering I didn't speak a word of Chinese at that stage, and he didn't speak any English at all. I managed to persuade him to become our driver. He really helped us a lot. I deliberately wanted a driver that did not speak English so that it would force me to learn Chinese, and it worked really well. Mr Huang was our driver for 4 years. I would chat with him every day, practicing what I had learnt with my Chinese teacher. It was really useful. He taught me a lot, especially getting the tones right. He eventually left to run the new canteen in the new factory I built. I used to tease him afterwards that he was a better cook than he was a driver. Though judging by the food in the canteen, that might have been true! Anyway, I was equally fortunate to replace Mr Huang with another great guy, Mr Fang. He was another really solid guy with a great attitude and we quickly became good friends. My Chinese was much better by then of course, so we could continue my conversational practice every day in the car. It was 25 minutes into work each way and so over the years I got plenty of Chinese conversation practice with these guys. I could not have done it without them. These guys became my best teachers and my best friends.

DR ANDY WYNN

CHAPTER 2

INTO THE AIRPOCALYPSE (OR DISCOVERING OUR NEW HOME)

Chinese cities are full of high rise living, not surprising given the population density, it's the only way to fit everyone in. Tall apartment blocks are the norm in all city centres and suburbs, with continuous building work going on to extend the city boundaries all the time. Shortly after we arrived, the intense economic growth that supported all this property building flattened, and it was not long before most of this building work ground to a halt. But fast forward 2 or 3 years, and growth was back on track and most of these half-finished projects were picked up where they left off. But even in a city like Dalian, there was just so many projects around that it was hard to imagine where all the people were going to come from to fill up these thousands upon thousands of new apartments. In just my short drive from the airport back home into the heart of the city, dozens of new apartment buildings were being erected. Given the height and number of tower blocks in each new community being built, I estimated that each one would be enough new living space to house up to 10,000 people, and I passed around 10 of these projects in just a 25 minute drive. That's 100,000 people that the government were expecting to move into the city centre. Not to mention the 3 times that amount they had been building near the waterfront, and the 10 times that they had been building out in the suburbs. That's over a million more people the city was gearing up to house, with all the infrastructure and local services that need to be there to support them all. Just where are all these people going to come from?

It's not surprising that many of these places still stand empty. Not quite ghost towns, as there has never been anyone living there to leave any ghosts, more like 'stalled' towns, expectant but as yet unborn, waiting for life to emerge. And beyond these dead spots in every city, there are entire 'stalled' cities spread out across China. It is estimated there are around 50 such cities, originally built to support growing industrial hotspots around the country. Now the vast majority of these 'stalled' cities lie largely empty, with parks, shopping malls and apartment blocks all waiting for families to arrive. This frantic building program across the country has been on a scale not seen before on Planet Earth. Over the last 30 years, the area of built up land in China has increased more than 5 times. Just think of how much concrete, steel and glass is needed to construct all those buildings. In just the three years between 2011 and 2013, China used more concrete than the whole of the United States used throughout the entire 20th Century. It is no wonder that the Chinese economy has reached a massive scale so quickly, with China at its peak accounting for half or more of the total world production of steel and concrete. And all of this stuff is not just for building housing. This mega industrial output also goes into building the mega-infrastructure projects that have littered the international press in recent years. Mega-dams, unbelievably big bridges, an ever extending rail network, longer and deeper road tunnels, the list goes on. The scale and vision is incredibly impressive and these mega-projects regularly break records for the biggest, longest, deepest… in the world. And there are plenty more on the drawing board.

And Dalian has its fair share, with the Dalian-Yantai Tunnel project planning to construct an undersea tunnel to connect Dalian on the Liaoning Peninsula to Yantai on the Shandong Peninsula, crossing the Bohai Sea, at an estimated cost of 32 billion dollars. The tunnel will be over 120 kilometres long, with over 70% of it under water. This is more than double the length of the English Channel tunnel, which is the current longest undersea tunnel on Earth at 50km. And Dalian has already seen 14 billion dollars invested in a new Dalian to Harbin-Dalian High-Speed Railway, which opened whilst I was living there and is the world's first high-speed railway that can operate at the sub-zero temperatures of Harbin in the winter.

Such mega-projects have been the key to opening up the country, making previously isolated regions more habitable and more accessible. More recently, the challenge for the Chinese economy has been how sustainable is all this? And with the massive demand for high volumes of these commodities, what about all the cutting corners on quality and environmental controls that has ensued? Everyone knows about the infamous Beijing Smog. Where do you think that comes from? It's from all the big power stations burning coal and all the big steel works and other industry surrounding the city, and from the millions of motor vehicles on the streets. This is the price of such a rapidly growing economy over the last 30 years. I remember one of my first trips to Beijing, the smog was hanging around when I arrived into the airport and took a taxi to my hotel. But not so bad as I expected. I was a little surprised in the hotel when I got in the elevator. They had one of those LED TV screens announcing the time and the weather for today and forecast for tomorrow. But it was the first time I'd seen a public display that also had the pollution level displayed. The most damaging type of pollution is what is measured as PM2.5, which is the ultra-fine particulate matter that hangs in the air and is small enough to get deep into a person's lungs. In China, this is mostly created by ash residues from burning coal. A PM2.5 above 50 is considered unhealthy, and above 250 is considered hazardous to health.

I woke up the next morning and opened my curtains to be greeted with a solid wall of smog on the other side of the glass. It was so thick I could not see out of my windows at all, it was like someone had painted them with a thick grey paint, but not just grey, the smog had a sickly yellowish, chemical like tinge to it. I just thought at that moment 'this city is so sick'. And Beijing is by no means the worst place in China for pollution, just the most well-known. Beijing famously orders the closure of its power stations and surrounding industry if it wants blue skies for an important political event in the city. The government now has the power to close factories on the spot round the country if they are suspected of exceeding allowed emissions levels, and this actually happened to some of our competitors whilst I was in China.

Soon after my Beijing experience I decided to add a pollution app to my phone to augment the weather apps.

Interesting watching the pollution maps of China. The most polluted air hangs around the northern industrial areas, particularly the big coal and steel producing regions. But the weather moves the pollution clouds around of course causing the effects to be felt from Mongolia down to South Korea, and even creating acid rain problems over in Seoul and Tokyo. To put the problem into context, it is said that air pollution in China contributes to the premature deaths of more than 300,000 people every year, and reduces the average Chinese lifespan by over three years. It was a common conversation piece amongst expats about just how much we were shortening our lives for every year we stayed in China.

In big cities it is common to see people walking around with masks on to combat the effects of air pollution. This is something you just don't see back home, and is something of a shock when you first arrive in China, though most of the masks you see people wearing are pretty useless in terms of actually blocking the damaging fine particulates. The wearing of masks is so common place that a whole industry has grown up to offer ever more fashionable dust mask alternatives to the standard industrial designs. And there are even special masks available for those hardy souls who plan to go running outside during periods of bad pollution.

Even in Dalian we were not immune to the effects of the air pollution problem, and this for a place that is known in China as an eco-city. Dalian is regularly voted China's most liveable city thanks to its good climate, and clean air. But I guess everything is relative. It is noticeable living in Dalian that the often blue skies are not truly blue, not to a European who is used to the sapphire blue of the Mediterranean skies or is used to holidaying amongst the azure skies of the Pacific South Sea Islands, in Dalian they always have a hint of grey haze clouding them. And after living in Dalian for some time you get fooled into thinking that your blue skies are fabulous, it's only when you take a trip somewhere overseas again that you are reminded what a blue sky is supposed to look like. We had our fair share of smog problems during my tenure in the city, when the pollution blows down from the steel plants around Shenyang in the North or across from Beijing in the West. There have been days when the sun was blocked so badly by pollution, with thick grey smog of PM2.5 above 1200 for several days. The kind of days that your phone app tells you it is not safe to exercise outside. I recall I had organised tennis with a friend in one of those days and was a little reluctant to go ahead given the conditions. But because it had taken weeks to lock down both of our diaries, we went ahead. Even though we played indoors, you could still see that the air hanging at the top of the tennis court was unusually grey and cloudy, like the tennis courts had their own microclimate, very weird. We probably took another year off our lives for playing the two hours under those conditions.

I have also experienced serious smog issues in other cities in China. I attended one big business meeting in Shanghai when the smog was so bad you couldn't see more than 10m in front of you. The drive from the airport was particularly hazardous that day. It was a big international meeting for our business, so we had a lot of colleagues flying in. For many it was their first time into Shanghai and for some of them, their first time in China. I felt really sorry for them, as they were there for 3 days, many had flown a long way to get there, and the smog never lifted the whole time. They arrived and left without seeing any of the famous sights of Shanghai, not even the towers of Pudong.

The government has realised that this can't go on any

longer and that's why it is cracking down on pollution big time now and investing so heavily in clean coal technologies and renewable energy. It already has the biggest wind turbine fields and solar energy farms on the planet, and is the biggest electric vehicle market. The Chinese government have introduced very tough new environmental policies. The challenge they have ahead of them is getting a lid on their pollution problems whilst at the same time maintaining economic growth. It hopes to achieve this by using its green policies to refocus its economy on becoming a leader in technological innovation. Hence we are seeing a shift in China from industries like steel production to electronics, biotechnology, and software and this is happening very quickly compared to how long the same shift happened in the West. This is all part of the same pattern of economic maturity we have seen historically in the West, it's just with China it is happening much, much quicker.

High rise living takes some getting used to if like me you came from a country where people live in single houses, with a garden front and back. It was quite an adjustment for us to make. But I quickly learnt to really enjoy city centre style living in a serviced apartment. No lawn to mow, no house maintenance to do, dozens of restaurants and bars on my doorstep, a gym, swimming pool and tennis courts just an elevator ride down, what's not to like!

There are many support services that have to be there to support all this high rise living. Not least of these is daredevil window cleaners. The first time we saw window cleaners hanging off ropes, and sitting on wooden planks 30 floors up, it was a scary, toe curling sight. But this is a regular sight in big cities, especially after Spring Festival, when all the apartment windows and building facades need a good scrub after the winter. Each column of windows has a guy dangling off a rope, meaning that typically there is a team of 5 or 6 dangling over the edge of one side of an apartment block at a time. They literally have one single rope, tied to a rough wooden plank which acts as their seat, with a bucket of water hanging off it. No harnesses, no safety gear, nothing to stop them face planting the concrete 100m below but their wits and a pair of tightly clenched buttocks. This must be one of the most dangerous jobs in the world. Maybe their arse is super glued to the plank. I know mine would be, but it wouldn't be super glue that was sticking me to the plank! Yes, the big cities with their new prestigious tourist drawing skyscrapers have Western style safety cradles for these guys, but out in real China, this just doesn't exist.

For 9 months of the year, living in Dalian is a real joy, with beaches, history, and great weather, but for the 3 months of winter, you quickly learn that Dalian has a down side. Our first winter in Dalian was horrific for us. Extreme cold by our standards, -20oC or below some days. Every trip out to the shops required a quick count of your ears when you got back home to check one hadn't dropped off in the cold. Our second winter was even worse, it was officially the coldest winter in China in 40 years. We thought, 'is it going to be like this every year'? The north wind that blows down from Russia was savage, so we soon learnt to buy all the right gear to keep warm and do like the locals and wrap our heads completely to keep our ears on. Living in the north of China has the advantage that all the large buildings have steam central heating, whereas there is nothing in the South. The practical consequence of this is that in Shanghai, you will be wearing your coat to the office and to dinner in the winter. Another challenge in winter is that all the shopping malls and restaurants are so hot but outside is so cold, so it's difficult to dress appropriately.

You're ether freezing cold or boiling hot. And the steam heating system in every office and apartment block in the North takes some getting used to. Every winter I had to walk around in my underpants in the apartment sweating whilst outside everything was solid with ice.

There are many things you take for granted back home. Back home you just know how to do stuff, and where to go to get things done. When you move to a new place in your home country you have to learn all this anew, but when you move to China, you first have this impenetrable great wall of Chinese language to get past before you can make any progress with anything. You need a lot of hand holding by Chinese colleagues and friends throughout your whole time there. One such thing you miss when moving to China, that you take for granted back home, is ordering stuff off the internet. Where is Amazon? Where is eBay? They do not exist. Chinese has all of its own versions of these sites, all in Chinese, no English. When you first open these sites up and the screen is just covered with tiny Chinese characters, it is seriously bewildering. You look for the English version on the site, no luck. You look for alternative English language sites in China, no luck. You resign yourself to the fact that if you really want to buy stuff over the internet you are going to have to dive in and work it all out. I made the wise choice of asking my Chinese teacher to help me. She spent an hour showing me around TaoBao (the Chinese equivalent of eBay) and JD.com (a massive online store specialising in electronics), really useful. It is a significant challenge ordering things in Chinese on the internet, but when you can do it, you really feel like you have achieved something. Working your way around the screens is a great source of entertainment and you feel like you are learning a useful skill. And the feeling of accomplishment when your goods arrive is great.

The whole internet experience is a challenge for a Westerner in China. You inevitably try to look for things in English on the internet, which gives you a big disadvantage when you're on the wrong side of the great firewall of China. This is not so bad in the Tier 1 cities, but moving to Dalian in 2011 was like moving back in time 20 years in many ways. The internet in our apartment was still plug in, wired and seriously slow. A source of great frustration for us for the first 2 years, but there were friends in our apartment block who were doing IT and finance jobs and needed good quality internet to do their work, to work with big spreadsheets and sync files with offices and colleagues across the world. I felt really sorry for them. We paid for a dedicated internet line when we moved in, but this was no better than the apartment internet, a real waste of money. But like everything else over the 6 years, it did get better, and eventually our Wi-Fi was okay, not great, but okay. I certainly noticed a major difference in internet speed whenever I travelled overseas.

There are several things that are always working against you as a foreigner in China on the internet. Firstly, the hardware. You read that China is investing massively in internet infrastructure, so why is your internet still so bad? Well, I have news for you, they are investing in infrastructure for their own citizens, not for us lǎowài's. If you want to access overseas websites, then all traffic is basically channelled through an undersea cable that runs under the Pacific Ocean. This hardware has a finite bandwidth, so the more foreigners try to access overseas website, the more it will slow down. This is the number one reason why your internet slows down every time Europe and the US wake up. Secondly, the censorship. The Chinese government has huge departments of people sitting monitoring the internet 24 hours a day and they are particularly sensitive to foreign traffic. Every time you log on, there is someone looking over your shoulder at what you are searching for online, at the content you are viewing, and the things you are posting. The government has very tight control over its internet. This is why all your foreign web services, like Google, Facebook, Twitter and Instagram, are blocked, and why the Chinese equivalents have risen to such prominence. And this is why China has the largest number of journalists and bloggers in prison in the world, because they are constantly searching for politically sensitive comments on line. So be warned. Thirdly, the VPNs. Because of the censorship and the blocking of access to key overseas websites, everyone resorts to using a VPN (Virtual Private Network). There are many on offer and they all have their pros and cons. A VPN has become an essential tool for every foreigner living in China. It gives you access to all those things online that you would otherwise be cut off from, like Facebook. But the Chinese government has long grown wise to this and is developing ever more sophisticated methods to block VPNs. That's why you need more than one VPN on your computer, because you can be using one and merrily working away and then everything suddenly cuts off, because the censors have overpowered the VPN software. So you have to change your settings and switch VPNs. This is just a constant battle when you are sitting in China. The government has also recently made it illegal for businesses to use VPNs and there is talk that this will be extended to personal use in the future. All of this means that trying to access overseas website while sitting in China is a constant battle ground and all the fiddling about with settings, and waiting for downloads, is one of the most massive wastes of your time in China.

If you are a Chinese person, sitting in China, searching

the Chinese internet in Chinese language, then no problem, it can be super-fast. The rise of internet TV and movie streaming services have wiped out the classic knock off DVD stalls that used to be on every street corner in only 2 or 3 years. When we first moved to Dalian, the only way to get to watch English language movies was to go and buy a knock off DVD from a back street vendor, and there were dozens of places to choose from. The quality of the knock offs varied tremendously, with around 30% unwatchable, but most were good enough to enjoy. Like most expats, we built up a huge collection of DVDs over the years. Not difficult when they are only 10 RMB a pop. I am not a great fan of knock offs, and I have and would never download music illegally, but in China at the time, there was just no alternative to the knock off DVDs. There were so many knock off stalls, that no legitimate shop sold real DVDs at all. I would literally have no clue where to go to buy a genuine DVD in China, so need's must.

Today's reality is that the World Wide Web is rapidly becoming split into two. Two internets are emerging, the English language US-led internet, and the Chinese language system led by the Chinese government. If you are not able to read and write Chinese, if you cannot type Chinese into Băidù (the Chinese equivalent of Google), then you are effectively locked out of the Chinese internet. You will be unable to keep up with local and national news, with local events, with social media, cutting you off from the real local community and reinforcing your existence in China as just part of a foreign expat community. Translation software is getting better and better, and I love the Chrome online translation feature, but it is still not good enough to solve this problem for you. So if you are a Westerner sitting in China, your internet experience will always be massively suppressed unless you just get on and learn some Chinese.

Beyond the partly self-inflicted challenges of the internet for expats, the speed at which China has embraced the digital age has been incredible to watch. When we arrived, China was still lagging behind the US in tech supremacy, but in just a few short years, China has been engulfed by a digital tsunami, touching every aspect of daily life, not just for professionals and the younger tech-savvy generation, but for all ages and strata of society. As mentioned before, China's virtual analogues of Google, eBay, Facebook, etc. have been cleverly ring-fenced by government policy, and tech entrepreneurship has been allowed and encouraged to grow at an unprecedented pace. Nowhere is the success of this policy more apparent than in China's shining jewel of the modern digital era, WeChat. WeChat began as a simple messaging app in 2011 by the company Tencent, the Chinese equivalent to WhatsApp. It quickly grew in capability and functionality to become a multi-purpose messaging, social media and mobile payment app, cleverly hanging off the coat tails of the parallel rise in smartphone ownership. By 2018 it was one of the world's largest standalone mobile apps, with over 1 billion monthly active users. WeChat is a fantastic example of the far reaching changes that can be achieved in the behaviours of an entire population in just a short time, if you have the vision, a no barriers attitude and a willing consumer playing field. Today, WeChat rules people's lives. You can pay your household bills, you can order home delivery food, order a taxi, buy movie tickets, buy train tickets, trade in stocks and shares, pay your tax bill, hire a bike, etc., etc. all from the convenience of one super integrated app. In the West you would have to open multiple different apps to do all these different things. And WeChat is adding more services all the time. For those of us that have lived through the rise of WeChat, moving back to the West and using WhatsApp just seems such a massive downgrade.

The number one practical change that WeChat has had on people's lives is WeChat Pay. In 2011, when we arrived in China, life on the street was still very much a hard cash economy. We would have to go everywhere armed with our bundle of 100 RMB notes (the biggest denomination) to pay for stuff in shops, taxis, bars and markets. And you would always end up collecting piles of useless tiny value coins. I had a great big jangling collection to get rid of after 6 years. Credit and debit cards could be used of course but the smaller local businesses preferred hard cash, some of them because dealing in cash gave them the opportunity to avoid paying VAT. Over the next 5 years, this slowly changed with the expanding use of WeChat Pay, to the point that when we left China, life on the street had completely transformed from a hard cash economy to a no cash economy. Now no one carries cash, because everywhere displays a QR code for paying by WeChat Pay. A simple scan with your smartphone transfers money from your account to the vendor's in an instant. What could be simpler, no cash, no pockets of change. Walking round a back street fruit and vegetable market today, every single local market stall has a piece of paper with a QR code taped to their stall so you can pay for your purchases with WeChat Pay. There are also QR codes hanging in taxis for paying your fare. Every corner shop has their QR code prominently displayed right next to their till. I am convinced that in a few more years' time, there will not even be a till at the checkout. What an amazing transformation in only a few years. There are other payment apps of course, but none of them have had the incredible impact and taken over China like WeChat.

One of the things I loved about living in Dalian is how beautifully the main streets and public areas are maintained.

If you were out very early for a crack of dawn flight, you were always guaranteed to see some of the army of public workers that the local government employ that are busy cleaning the streets, planting flowers in the middle of the main streets, tending the flower beds in the public gardens, setting up lights for public events everywhere, etc. I'm sure many of these were very poorly paid, but there was a lot of them. During the main public holidays, there was always miles upon miles of pretty lights tracing down the streets. In the winter, driving the 25 minutes from the airport back home, all the roads we drove down were festooned with lights the whole way along. The magnificent Xinghǎi square, the largest public space in the city, and the jewel of the tourist area, was always totally resplendent and pristine whatever the time of year, particularly around the big festivals. It was really nice to see where your tax dollars went. We all have to pay taxes, it's never popular but you just have to put up and pay up. But it was a good feeling in Dalian seeing your tax dollars so visible in all the city landscaping and winter lights, you felt you were getting something directly back for it. This is in total contrast to when I lived in the UK, where paying taxes feels like you get little value for your hard earned tax money. There is an overwhelming feeling that your money is disappearing into a black hole, and being squandered on illegal immigrants and scroungers.

Xinghǎi square is not only the largest public square in Asia, but at 110 hectares, is the largest public square in the whole world. Xinghǎi means Star Sea, or Sea of Stars, in Chinese. It was built in 1998 to commemorate the centenary of the founding of the modern city of Dalian. In 2011, when we arrived in the city, it was an incredible and impressive place to visit, a vast open green space, littered with sculptures, surrounded by high end restaurants, convention & exhibition centres, and with a tourist bay front area. Since then, building work in the surrounding area has continued, extending the facilities tremendously.

At the centre of the square is a large circular marble platform with the signs of the Chinese zodiac engraved into the floor. It is a common sight to see tourists walking around and around looking for their particular sign. In the exact centre of the platform was a giant 20m high 'huábiǎo', which is type of traditional ceremonial column. The most famous and recognisable huábiǎo are to be seen at Tiananmen Square in Beijing. The Dalian huábiǎo was erected in 1997 to commemorate China's resuming sovereignty over Hong Kong and was notable as the tallest huábiǎo in China. It quickly became a symbol of the city, and was always instantly recognisable and associated with Xinghǎi square. During one night in August 2016 it was demolished in secret by the local government, causing uproar from local people. The local government were tight lipped about their reasons and local and national media reports were suppressed. I heard on the grapevine that it was demolished because it was set up by the then mayor of Dalian, Bo Xilai, an infamous name in China, as he was one of the first major high profile arrests during the government crackdown on corruption in 2013, so fell quickly out of favour.

The centre platform of the square is surrounded by huge swathes of grass areas and landscaped borders, hiding a criss-cross of access roads. Beyond that, joining the square to the bay front tourist area is the city's centennial sculpture, which displays 1000 footprints walking out towards the sea, down the middle of a ginormous open book. The book sculpture is regularly full of tourists trying to walk up to the edge of the book, which gets so high and so steep that it is almost impossible to walk to the end,

There is a red line on the floor about a metre from the edge to warn people of the dangerous drop, but this does not deter many people. But even I found it difficult to walk right to the edge, as your ankles really struggle with the near vertical angle there. The gentle slope in the middle, curving slowly ever steeper towards the two edges of the book make it a perfect launch point for roller skaters and skate boarders, like a huge wide half pipe. So walking around this area always requires keeping an eye open to avoid crashing into one of the gangs of Chinese youth that skate around showing off their skills.

Xinghǎi Square has been a centrepiece of the city's festivals and events ever since it first opened. There was an annual Chinese New Year firework display held there until the government banned the use of fireworks in major cities a couple of years ago, in an effort to control pollution. Every summer there is a 10 day International Beer Festival held in the square, with large marquees erected to house the drunken revellers and Bavarian-style Oompah bands.

The bay front area itself is always full of couples and families, enjoying all the usual stuff that aims to keep tourists happy; food and gift stalls, little rides for the kids, bicycles and roller skates for hire. There is a beach to the eastern end of this zone. In the winter it is always amusing to watch the local swimmers braving the icy waters of the sea from this beach. These guys are made from strong stuff. Xinghǎi Square even has its own amusement park, in the far corner of the area, forming one end of the bay front tourist zone. We wandered through it on several occasions, a lovely atmosphere in the evening with all the lights on and the noises and laughter of a fair. We even tried a handful of the rides, though there is something special about going on a Chinese fairground ride. There is definitely an extra element of risk that you feel regarding the level of maintenance and testing that the hulking great rusty mechanism that you are strapping yourself into has seen recently. I always wonder if the screams of the riders are the reason I don't hear any groans from the bearings as they spin round at high speed. I'm okay with most types of rides, but the one that really gets me is that Pirate Ship. When you're sitting at the back row and you're end is right up in the air, perpendicular to the ground and all you're looking at is the other end of the ship with all the people screaming, that's when my stomach squeezes so tight I think it's going to squeeze the contents straight back up out of my mouth. That feeling as the ship whips down and pulls the g's gives me a nauseating squeal deep in the pit of my bladder. Blaaargh!

Another incredible piece of engineering that we witnessed the construction of during our time in Dalian was the new Xinghǎi Bay Bridge. This opened officially to traffic in October 2016, but we saw it grow from a few tiny concrete stubs poking out of the water into a giant of a suspension bridge over 5 years. It spans the whole of the bay area, linking the centre of Dalian with the suburbs towards LǔShùn, allowing commuters to bypass the city centre, saving 40 minutes' drive time, and allowing tourists to get a magnificent view of the whole Xinghǎi Square area. Although it does seem a design fault that if the planners wanted tourists to see the view from the bridge, there is no stopping allowed on the bridge, though this doesn't stop people of course, and an impromptu car park always builds up on the bay side of the bridge as cars and tourist buses stop for eager tourists to take a few pictures of the wonderful views. The bridge is the first anchor suspension oversea bridge in China, with a total sea span of 6.8 kilometres, with 8 lanes for traffic, 4 over and four under, as it is a split level design to allow for high volumes of two way traffic. There is a pedestrian walkway across the whole of the length, which makes for a great Sunday morning walk.

There are also some notable buildings in and around the Xinghǎi square area, which really add to the atmosphere and world class feel of the whole district. When we arrived in 2011, the Dalian Shell Museum was housed high on a hill called Lotus Mountain, overlooking the square in a building shaped like a magnificent castle. This was a tremendously popular spot for couples wanting wedding photos, and there was always a queue of young couples up there waiting to get the best spots. A really romantic location and dream-like backdrop. This castle soon closed after we arrived though for extension and remodelling work, which spawned not one but two magnificent new buildings. Late in 2014 the castle finally reopened. Massively expanded, it had been transformed into an ultra-luxury Bavarian-style castle hotel, part of the Starwood chain. Inside, the public spaces were beyond opulent and the venue became popular amongst Julie's expat wives group as a great place for afternoon tea, enjoying the fabulous views across the bay. Every time I flew on any flight in and around Asia during that time, I could not open any inflight magazine without there being a picture of this magnificent iconic new hotel inside. The hotel makes for an incredible impression when you first see it and has made a lasting impression on the landscape, adding positively to the whole ambience of the Xinghǎi Square area. As a business, the hotel has not been without its teething troubles, and whilst it might have looked glossy on the outside, our first restaurant experience there was pretty poor. We tried their new German restaurant, complete with their own on site microbrewery, with some friends, but the food and the service was frankly terrible, the worst experience in our whole 6 years in China.

The German restaurant closed soon after that. It seems odd that the hotel would spend billions on building such a magnificent hotel and then not train its staff properly. This was early days for the hotel and I'm sure it has all been put right since then. The second building that came from the closure of the original Shell Museum, was the brand new Shell museum. This was a completely new, purpose built design down in the square, next to the fairground. In contrast to the traditional design of the castle hotel, the new shell museum is an ultra-modern concept, with the whole building designed to look like a vast magnificent shell, using the latest in steel cladding materials to create a natural appearance with huge flowing curves. Inside, the museum displays more than 5,000 types of shells from all over the world. Not something that I would normally rush to see, but I was definitely up for a visit once it opened just to experience the building up close, and I wasn't disappointed. Though I have to say, the interior is really cleverly designed to mimic the inside of a big shell, winding you slowly up 4 floors to the very apex, where there are great views of the area to be had. And the whole experience, including the shells themselves, was far more interesting than I had imagined, definitely worth a visit. Strolling round the colourful shell displays, with so many weird and wonderful shapes, reminded me of wandering round an art gallery, such is the range of imaginative colours, textures and designs on display.

Whilst I'm on the subject of new buildings, I have to mention the new Grand Hyatt hotel, built across the square, directly opposite from the Shell museum. It is a modern tower design, and the tallest hotel in the area. Since it opened in 2015 it transformed our expat social scene because of the great restaurants, the perfect location and the wonderful staff (a special thank you to Jim for looking after us so many times). The best restaurant in the city is now 'Dalian Dalian' on floor 44 of the Grand Hyatt. This serves the very best of North East Chinese cuisine and all against the backdrop of the awe inspiring views of Xinghǎi Square and bay. The views of the Bay Bridge at night are just jaw dropping. With the opening of this restaurant, Dalian finally had a place to take visitors that had that WOW factor. I entertained many, many colleagues, visitors and friends there over the last two years and every single one said the same thing to me. First timers to the 'Biggest City they had Never Heard of' were expecting Dalian to be a low grade, backward place that had yet to catch up with the Shanghai's and Beijing's of the world, and so were stunned when I took them to 'Dalian Dalian' for dinner to enjoy the views, they 'never imagined it would be like this'. People also said to me that they finally understood why I liked living here. We regularly hosted work dinners and events in the 'Dalian Dalian' private rooms, and must have spent a lot of money there over the years, but it was all worth it. It got even better once the hotel opened its high rise bar 'Viva' on floor 46, a great place for late night vibes and after dinner drinking into the small hours. We were there on the opening night. Julie pulled a few strings and got us in to the party (she knows everyone!).

DR ANDY WYNN

CHAPTER 3

UNDER MORTAR ATTACK (OR PUBLIC HOLIDAYS IN CHINA)

The first time I experienced a Public Holiday in China was quite an odd event. Like everything else in your daily life that you do in China, they have to put their own special twist on it. There was a two day public holiday off work coming up soon, way hey! I don't remember the particular festival or event this was commemorating, there are plenty of new ones to get used to for a Westerner. I asked my Chinese colleagues which days it was, and the conversation went something like this;

Me; Which days are the public holidays later this week?
Them; Friday and Saturday.

Me; Friday and Saturday? But hang on, we don't work on a Saturday anyway, so it's only one day holiday in

reality, so why say its two days holiday? So we come back to work on Monday then?
Them; No, we have to come into work on Sunday to make up for the Friday off.

Me; Are you kidding me? We have to work on Sunday to compensate for the public holiday we took on Friday? Are you serious?
Them; Yes

Me; So we don't really have any public holiday at all this weekend. All they are doing is shifting the work days around a bit.

My Chinese colleagues of course did not really see it like that because this is just normal for them. What I saw was that we had to work 4 days one week and 6 days the following week. What's the point of that? If we have to work at the weekend to make up for a day off in the week, surely that's not really a holiday then! They just shifted the weekend. But this is yet another example of China challenging my fixed Western concepts of how things should be done. This Chinese concept of a public holiday is in complete contrast to the approach in the West, where Friday and Monday national holidays are things which people really look forward to because they give them an opportunity for the fabled 'long weekend'. The Chinese public holiday calendar is littered with such pseudo-holidays that aren't really holidays at all. What is that all about? And to layer confusion on top of bewilderment, whilst some of these public holidays published by the national government are truly national and obligatory, many are at the discretion of the provincial government. Our provincial government in Dalian only seemed to make these discretionary public holiday decisions the day before the scheduled holiday date, and being the lǎowài, I was always the last to hear. This did not making planning my life very easy.

But it's all swings and roundabouts of course. The way that the odd one or two day public holidays are sometimes messed around are compensated by the fact that China has two, week-long national holidays. Yes two! They have Chinese New Year at the end of January or start of February and a week-long national holiday in October to celebrate the founding of the People's Republic of China. Although these week-long holidays also suffer from some moving around of work versus pseudo public holidays, at least you do get a full 7 days continuously off work for each. Although one year we had to work a 9 day continuous stretch before hand to make up for some of the public holidays the following week.

I learnt quickly that one of the advantages of being an expat in China, is that you get the best of both worlds with your holidays. You are supposed to contractually go with the public holidays of your local country, and that essentially means in China, one week for Chinese New Year, plus one week for Chinese National Holiday week. Everything shuts down around these dates. So that essentially means, no Christmas holiday, and no long Calendar New Year holiday (China has just one day off). This is seriously weird for a Westerner. I remember the first year I was working in China, sat in the office on Christmas day, just a normal day at the office. That was very, very odd, but heh ho. After that first year, I soon discovered that as a Westerner in a global Western company, my job interacted with the global business, so since the rest of the world shut down for Christmas and New Year, it prevented me from doing a lot of my job. So I soon realised that I might as well take Christmas and New Year off as holiday as well. So I ended up every year with a long Christmas and New Year western style holiday, plus a long holiday around Chinese New Year and a long holiday around Chinese National Week. It was really great, and gave us lots of free time to travel around and explore Asia. The only problem was that since many of these were obligatory public holidays for Chinese, then if you actually wanted to fly anywhere and stay in nice hotels at the beach resorts of Asia, prices became sky high and availability was really low. Supply and demand; during Chinese New Year, millions of Chinese swarm around Asia for vacations, so prices shoot up. So although we got the holidays, it seriously cost us.

There are seven official national holidays in China every year, but of these, only two are shared with Western countries, namely the 1st January 'calendar' New Year's Day and 1st May Labour Day (or called May Day in some countries). The rest are built around the lunar calendar and Chinese historical events; Chinese New Year (Spring Festival), Qingming Festival, Mid-Autumn Festival, and National Day.

The first thing you have to get your head around with national holidays in China is the lunar calendar. Since in the West we use the Gregorian calendar, all our public holidays are fixed on the same date every year, so that is what we are used to. As the name suggests, the lunar calendar is based upon the cycles of the Moon, and how its phases change over a month. A solar calendar is based on following the annual cycles of the sun. The Gregorian calendar is a solar calendar system with a few minor tweaks to make the maths match up with the sun's movement, e.g. adding a leap year. China has used the Gregorian calendar since the first half of the 20th century, bringing it in line with the rest of the world, but still upholds its traditions based around the lunar calendar, which includes many of its public holidays. The practical result of this is that the dates for these holidays float around in the Gregorian calendar, even though they are fixed in the lunar calendar. Yet another great example of how China challenges even your concept of time and what a 'date' really is. I love it.

Chinese New Year, or Spring Festival, is the first of the big lunar calendar based festivals each year, and the biggest celebration of the whole year for the Chinese. It falls around the end of January or early in February. It's the closest thing in China to Christmas, or to Thanksgiving in the US, because it is a time for families to get together. The big family annual reunion dinner is traditionally held on the evening preceding Lunar New Year's Day. Families clean their houses top to bottom, similar to the annual 'Spring Clean' in the West, though it is said to be for sweeping away ill-fortune and making way for the incoming year's good luck. Doors will be decorated with red coloured paper-cuts of the Chinese character 'Fú' meaning good fortune, and with couplets that talk about happiness, wealth and long life. You can buy such things everywhere around this time, and every year we proudly displayed our Fú and couplets above the door to our apartment. But there is a trick to hanging your Fú, you are supposed to hang it upside down. This forms a Chinese wordplay on the phrase 'good luck arrives', and so translates into a wish for prosperity to descend upon the home.

Chinese New Year is also a time when parents hand out the famous Hóng Bǎo, or red envelopes containing money, to their children, although it isn't exclusively for Spring Festival, as it is also a practice for handing over money at weddings, births and graduations. In 2014, WeChat reinvented Hóng Bǎo for the modern age when they introduced the ability to send Hóng Bǎo via mobile payments via smartphone in 2014.

Spring Festival is also the cause of the famous annual mass migration of almost 400 million people that travel back home over a two or three day period for their family reunion dinner, causing the transport infrastructure to groan under the strain. Although the official New Year is one specific date (which changes every year of course), the Festival is marked by a week long holiday from work, where all businesses close down across the country (apart from shops, restaurants and hotels), but just like for Christmas in the UK, there is somewhat of a run up to the Festival, where business starts to slow down, and a slow return to work afterwards, so the 1 week Festival actually has a much longer influence across the country. The New Year itself is traditionally marked by letting off firecrackers, which can make for a very noisy day if you live in a big city.

The first time that Chinese New Year came round for us in China, we decided to stay in Dalian to experience the celebration. A new and exciting time for us. We had seen all the pomp and ceremony of Chinese cultural events plenty of times on the TV, with all the music, the colour and dancing, so we had high expectations. Never again.

We lived high on the 28th floor of our apartment building, on the main street of the financial district in Dalian. It was basically a long line of mini skyscrapers running the whole length, either side of the street. A great wind tunnel for those bitterly cold winters, like the Chinese equivalent of Chicago. We discovered that first Chinese New Year that this also had another unfortunate side effect. The first firecracker went off around 6am on the first day of the holiday. And when I say firecracker, I actually mean a huge box of industrial grade firecrackers, more like mini sticks of dynamite.

The Chinese certainly know how to make fireworks. I remember a few years back a news item on the TV about a delivery truck in Henan province loaded with fireworks that exploded and destroyed the bridge it was travelling on. The Chinese demand for fireworks always puts a strain on supply in the lead up to Chinese New Year, and most years there is some such incident reported surrounding the unsafe transport or storage of large quantities of fireworks.

The noise from the fireworks reverberated around our building, bouncing off the surrounding apartment blocks, and raising it to a window rattling crescendo. This sonic assault continued every few minutes throughout the day as new boxes of fireworks were lit outside stores, restaurants, and in the middle of side and main streets. This went on until midnight. What a day, but the fun was not over. Over the next few days everyone in the local vicinity seemed at some point to appear on the streets to make their own personal contribution to the Chinese New Year celebrations. The onslaught continued from six in the morning to midnight every day for the whole week. After 3 days I had more than had enough. This was not the fun celebration of Chinese culture that I expected, this felt more like we were under mortar attack. And it wasn't just the noise. The big boxes of firecrackers left loads of streams of red paper debris everywhere. Every street was awash with it, making a huge untidy mess, and looked like the streets were infected with some huge red mould. It took the authorities several days to clean up.

Chinese New Year is also when the famous Chinese zodiac signs come into play, as the day marks the start of the year for the 12 animal zodiac signs, which are in order; Rat, Ox, Tiger, Rabbit, Dragon, Snake, Horse, Goat, Monkey, Rooster, Dog, or Pig. Your Chinese Zodiac sign is derived from your birth year, according to the Chinese lunar calendar. People born in a specific animal year are believed to possess the attributes of that animal, personally, I am a Snake, which means that my main attribute is flexibility. There are several theories as to why the 12 Chinese Zodiac animals are in the order that they are. One theory suggests that the Jade Emperor called on all animals to help mankind and only 12 responded, another suggests a Great Race was held to determine which animals would be placed in the zodiac for eternity. Yet another suggests they are placed in order according to a mixture of the odd or even number of their feet, combined with Chinese Yin and Yang Theory. Whichever, it's all very confusing. Contrary to what you might expect, when your animal birth year comes round every 12 years, it is actually considered bad luck for you, for the whole year.

Qingming Festival, or Tomb Sweeping Day, is in early April each year and as the name suggests it focuses on the remembrance of departed family members. Family will visit their graves and pay respect by cleaning the gravestones and offering food and drink to their ancestors and burning ritual offerings. These offerings used to be traditional joss sticks but in modern times have got increasingly bizarre, as people started burning bundles of fake money, and even cardboard cut outs of iPhones and iPads. Although the day has long been observed for over 2,000 years, it only became an official public holiday in 2008, when the Chinese government revised the annual national holiday rota.

Dragon Boat Festival, or Duānwǔ Jié in Chinese, is a traditional holiday that falls on the 5th day of the 5th lunar month, which results in it floating around different dates within June each year. The festival commemorates the death of Qū Yuán, considered one of the greatest poets in Chinese history, who lived 340-278 BC, and has been held every year for the last 2,000 years. There are normally 3 pseudo-days off for this festival. It is particularly popular in the south, which is where you can see the famous Dragon Boat races going on around this time. Dragon boat racing originates from the tradition that Qū Yuán drowned himself on this day to avoid seeing his beloved state of Chu conquered by a neighbouring state, and people rowed their boats across the river to save him. Dragon Boat racing is really fun to watch and has grown into some big annual events, not only in the South of China, but also in some overseas countries. This festival is also associated across the country with eating zòngzi, which is a glutinous rice dumpling wrapped in leaves in a pyramid shape. They come with various sweet or savoury fillings depending on where you live around the country. In Dalian, zòngzi are quite subtle in taste but usually quite sweet and pretty good.

The Mid-Autumn festival, is celebrated every year on the 15th day of the 8th month of the lunar calendar, which falls around late September or early October, coinciding with a full moon. It is the second biggest lunar based festival after the Chinese New Year and is essentially the Chinese version of a Harvest festival. The festival is associated with mooncakes, which are on sale everywhere around this time. All the fancy shops, restaurants and hotels offer their own, all in exquisitely designed gift boxes, packaged for the giving of grand gifts to family members and business customers. The first time I tasted a moon cake I was distinctly underwhelmed. I had heard a lot about them and how you must try them. They come in different flavours with different savoury or sweet fillings, but every single one I have had tastes pretty bland to me. The best I had was one filled with nuts, but when I say 'best' I really mean the most tolerable. Not great and I wouldn't bother. After a couple of years I plucked up the courage to ask a few Chinese friends and colleagues about the Moon cake tradition. Most admitted to me that they don't like them themselves, and that these fancy boxes of moon cakes get given to family and passed round every year unopened, just like those unwanted gifts at Christmas. So what I have learnt about moon cakes is that the reality really does not live up to the hype. Sure try them once, they are not terrible, they are just bland, better to look at than to eat. And in my experience, the box tastes better than the mooncakes inside.

October 1st is Chinese National Day, held every year to commemorate the founding of the People's Republic of China, so the government puts on a lot of big events around this time across the country. October 1st is the start of 'Golden Week' as it gets drawn out into a full 7 day public holiday. As I said earlier, there is always a lot of travelling around these dates as the increasingly wealthy middle class take foreign holidays, pushing up hotel and flight prices considerably across Asia. It is also advisable to avoid all major tourist destinations in China during this period, as they get overwhelmingly busy. For those staying at home, many shopping malls traditionally offer big sales during Golden Week.

In addition to the seven national holidays, there are a host of other semi-official national and provincial festivals that may or may not be celebrated depending on where you live in China. There is a Women's Day, where ladies get half a day off work, plus a similar thing for Children's Day, where kids get a day off school.

The Chinese version of Valentine's Day is called the Qixi festival and falls on the 7th day of the 7th lunar month (and hence is sometimes called the Double Seven Festival). It's different from the Western version as the date is more about matchmaking than revealing your hidden love for someone and sending gifts. An interesting anti-Valentine's

Day event has grown up in China in recent years called Singles Day, which is on 11th November, i.e. 11/11. This was started in 1993 by students at Nanjing University as a day for single people to celebrate their single status. This concept was fuelled by clever marketing by Alibaba in 2009, into an annual event when single people are encouraged to spoil themselves and buy themselves a gift. Encouraged by 'Singles Day' discounts at online stores, it has since grown into the biggest online shopping day on the planet, bigger than America's Black Friday and Cyber Monday put together, and breaking its own record for online sales every year.

One of the more memorable semi-official national holidays is the Lantern Festival, held every year on the 15th day of the first calendar month. This marks the effective end of the Chinese New Year period. The evening is a very memorable and beautiful site in any major city square or Public Park, as families take their children out to release thousands of paper lanterns, always coloured red for good luck, into a night sky emblazoned with the full moon. Glutinous rice balls, sweet sticky treats, are traditionally eaten on this day.

I discovered another annual event that I never knew anything about one morning whilst sitting in my office. It was 18th September 2012, a Tuesday, I had been living in Dalian almost one year. It was 9:18 am when the air raid sirens went off all over the city. I looked round at my colleagues, and no one turned a hair. 'What's this? Should we do something?' I asked. What they told me was an eye opener for me. Air raid sirens are sounded at 9:18 am on 18th September across the whole of the northeast to commemorate the 'Manchurian Incident' which was the launch of a Japanese invasion of the region in 1931. It took the Japanese only a few months to take control of the northeast, as the Chinese government decided to retreat to the south and compromise their territory for the sake of peace, allowing the Japanese to set up their own state in place of Manchuria, which they called Manchukuo. The millions of Chinese that lived in the area suffered terribly during the 1930s under Japanese occupation, and hence why there is still such an anti-Japanese sentiment amongst the Chinese even today. In 1937, Japan initiated a full-scale invasion into the rest of China. The Chinese call this the 'People's War of Resistance against Japanese Aggression'. Early on in the conflict was the infamous Nanjing Massacre, where Japanese troops killed more than 300,000 Chinese people, including civilians, over a six-week period. The eight-year war that followed, cost more than 36 million Chinese lives and only ended with Japan's surrender at the end of World War 2 in 1945. The air raid sirens that sound every year, last for three minutes, to give people time to reflect on the events. I had never really appreciated this part of China's history before. I'd kind of heard about conflicts between Japan and China in the past but never really paid much attention to it. It was the other side of the planet after all and didn't really seem to have any bearing on me.

One of the benefits of living in a completely different country on the other side of the world from where you grew up, is that you get to learn about completely different versions of history, both in terms of histories new to you and in terms of hearing about histories you already know something about but told from a completely different point of view. This also plays out in current affairs. It was really eye opening sitting at home in our apartment in China watching news on the TV. We had access to TV news from different countries, and it was very revealing listening to US, UK and Chinese news channels report on the same events. The different points of view and the way different facts were presented, really brought it home to us that spin and propaganda are rife everywhere, and that all countries are as bad as each other for this. There were also times when your overseas news programme would inexplicably go blank when they were about to discuss some politically sensitive item related to China. So censorship is sure alive and well in China.

Dalian and the whole Liaoning province has a really rich modern history that is different from the rest of China, which makes the look and feel of the city quite unique in the country. Over the last 100+ years, the area has been under the various control of Britain, Russia and Japan at different times, mixing many different cultural and architectural influences with the native Chinese. The period of Russian control was due to them leasing the area from the Chinese government as they wanted access to the nearby ice free port of LǔShùn, unique at these latitudes as it was ice free year round. Russia's major port in the region was Vladivostok, but this was only accessible, and ice free, during the summer. LǔShùn is an hour west of Dalian and has always been a place of strategic naval importance, due to it fantastic natural harbour and so has a rich military history. In the past it was called Port Arthur by the British. It is still a very important harbour for the Chinese navy, as they have their fleet of nuclear submarines located there. You can get a great view of them all lined up in their pens from across the bay, on top of báiyùshān (white jade hill), one of the key tourist viewpoints of the area. The period of Russian control, saw a war between Russia and Japan, played out on Chinese soil, as the two countries fought for dominance over the whole of the North East Asia region. Today, this historical hot pot makes for some interesting war tourism in and around Dalian and LǔShùn. Dalian's Modern museum has a whole section on the Japanese occupation, interesting if you like seeing old guns and military uniforms. LǔShùn has a number of fascinating and eerie war sites to visit, including a Russian-Japanese prison, and a fortress on a hill with lots of old weapons from the decades of modern conflict in the area. We visited LǔShùn a handful of times over our 6 years living in Dalian, and it was always a memorable visit with new things to explore. We went a couple of times as part of tour groups organised by a local tour company. One visit was particularly memorable. They took us to visit a decommissioned nuclear submarine, not normally something open to foreigners. As an important military port in China, much of the area around the naval base is closed to foreigners and you are at risk of arrest if you wander into the wrong area. As part of the official tour group, we were given special access to naval tourist areas only usually available to Chinese nationals and at the end of the tour we found out just how much it is aimed exclusively at the Chinese. The submarine itself was interesting, but I'm sure it was an old one if they let us crawl around inside. The submarine was parked next to a specially constructed tourist complex, the main feature of which was a submarine dive simulation. We were all marched into this large room, kitted out like the control room of a submarine, except of course for the large area that allowed about 40 of us tourists to stand behind, surrounded by TV screens and projectors to look like window views out of a submarine, with water lapping at the screens. The screens showed an animated view of the Chinese naval base in front of us, complete with the other submarines parked in their pens. No one questioned that such windows wouldn't actually be in a submarine, but I guess that would spoil the fun. There were three 'crew' manning the control room and they took us all through a simulated dive, barking out orders, whilst the surrounding screens showed us diving down from LǔShùn bay and travelling under water for a spell, watching the seabed, and animated sharks and whales glide past the screens. What happened next shocked and stunned even me and I am pretty unflappable.

After five minutes or so travelling under water, we resurfaced. Ahead of us on the horizon were the Diàoyú Islands. These uninhabited islands lie between China, Taiwan and Japan and ownership has long been disputed between these nations. They are known as the Senkaku Islands by Japan. They have been under Japanese control for the whole of the last century, but questions over their sovereignty began to surface in the 1970s when the existence of oil reserves were revealed (who would have thought!). On the screens ahead of us were several naval ships, all flying Japanese flags and displaying Japanese logos on their hulls. The 'crew' pretended to survey the area and picked out one of the vessels, and then proceeded to go through a simulated torpedo arming and launching. I watched shocked as the torpedo ran through the water straight at the Japanese ship they'd targeted and proceeded to blow the thing out of the water. The animation showed a huge explosion and the sinking of the vessel. As I stood dazed by what I had witnessed, they did all of this again, sinking another vessel. I was stunned by this whole episode. I stood open-mouthed as we dived back down under the sea and headed back to the naval harbour at LǔShùn. I kept looking around the crowd. No one batted an eye, as if this was all terribly normal. I was stunned by such an amazing piece of political showmanship and propaganda masquerading as a tourist visitor centre. You have normal families and their kids being shown the sinking of another nations vessels as if it is normal and okay. I'm sure there were no Japanese people in the crowd. Can you imagine this in the UK or the US? Can you imagine a US submarine diving down in the simulation only to arrive at one of the South Sea Islands to blast a Chinese boat out of the water? There would be uproar, people would get prosecuted and probably go to prison if such a tourist attraction was set up.

After the amazing submarine incident, we were all frogmarched off to another site, where we got to visit some old disused cannons, decades old, on a ridge overlooking the bay. Interesting and a great view, but the disturbing thing was, to get up to the hill, we had to walk past the existing naval barracks and we were told we had to look the other way as we walked because if we were seen looking at the barracks or taking a picture, we would get arrested. That certainly adds a touch of spice to your relaxing day out sightseeing.

In a completely different capacity, the Chinese navy played a small but important part of my life in China almost daily for my first couple of years there. Dalian is an important ship building port and also has a naval presence in the harbour. Every day when I drove from my apartment to the office, I would pass the naval shipyard. I had the privilege to watch China's very first aircraft carrier, the Liaoning, being fitted out every day from a distance, when I went to work and back. This was a complete surprise to me at first because I hadn't heard about this vessel. When I did some digging, I found out that this was actually an ex-Soviet ship, built in 1985, and although sea worthy, it was never fully combat fitted because of the collapse of the Soviet Union in 1991. The stripped down hulk was purchased by the Chinese navy in 1998 and towed to the

Dalian naval shipyard, where it was slowly rebuilt. It was officially commissioned in September 2012 and I remember seeing the aircraft carrier sailing down the harbour bedecked with flags that morning on my daily commute. During its first few sea trials, its focus was as a training ship to get the Chinese navy used to the operation and capabilities of an aircraft carrier. After several returns to Dalian and subsequent refits, it was eventually announced as fully combat ready in November 2016, where it promptly left for a tour of duty down in the South China Sea. When I first saw the aircraft carrier I didn't actually know what it was, because it was hidden behind some giant grey panels. I asked around and was told what was going on, and that the panels were a bit pointless because the vessel was on the landing flight path of the local airport, so anyone could look inside the panelling every time they flew into Dalian airport. When the panelling was first removed to prepare for the first sea trails at was quite a peculiar site for my Western eyes. I was used to seeing a US style aircraft carrier, with a completely flat surface for the aircraft to take off and land, but this had what looked like a massive ski slope extending out into the front of the vessel, quite weird if you've never seen one before. Anyway, it was a very interesting experience to see it every day getting built.

DR ANDY WYNN

CHAPTER 4

BARGAINING FOR COMIC BOOK HAIRDOS (OR THE PERILS OF SHOPPING IN CHINA)

The whole shopping culture in China is another change of pace for a Westerner from a small town in the UK. When you're living in a big city, shops are everywhere and stay open late every night, making for ultra-convenience, mega-choice and a never ending stream of bright lights and colourful characters to people watch. Julie tells me I am not like most men, because I love shopping. But what I love is not the buying stuff, it's all the life spilling out on the street and in the shopping malls. I find the constant flow and buzz of people wandering round invigorating, and ten times so in China as everything is so new and strange and exotic. A successful shopping trip for me does not have to end in a purchase, and many is the time I come back home empty handed but satisfied. A shopping trip for me is a leisure activity, an opportunity to stretch my legs and in China, an opportunity to broaden my horizons. The snippets of conversation you hear are great tests for your Chinese language skills, the way people interact and the fashions they wear are great ways to learn about the alien culture you have plonked yourself in the middle of.

Some of the new fashion styles you see on the street are great fun and challenge you to try on a few new styles yourself in the shops, but after many, many try-ons and a few purchases, I have come to the conclusion that Asian styles only really look good on Asians. It's much to do with body shapes. As a middle aged, average sized Western guy, I would struggle to find anything that fit me in the shops. It wasn't so much on height, it was mainly on width. The Caucasian frame is naturally wider than an Asian frame and since all the shirts and trousers are cut for the Asian market, I would constantly struggle to find shirts that fit my chest and trousers big enough for my waist. Even Western high street chain shops in China are catering for the local Chinese market, so do not hold stock specifically for Westerners. So buying new off the peg clothes was a constant challenge in China. I think on average that for every twelve items I would try on, one fitted well enough to buy it. The only exception from all this was Uniqlo, which is a huge Japanese clothing chain. There are a few of their shops in the West, but they are all over Asia. Uniqlo became my go to life saver, as their XL size fitted me perfectly. It was the only shop I never had to try clothes on because I knew they would be a perfect fit for me. So I quickly became 'man at Uniqlo' during my time in China.

The influence of Western fashion was definitely noticeable in China. I thought it very strange that as you walk around the city, all the advertising for clothes stores everywhere shows only western people. Very rare to find one with a Chinese or Asian model in the photo. Even in the shops, the music you hear piped through is always familiar Western songs. In fact, I found myself deliberately going in to some stores, not to buy any clothes, but just to listen to the music. Some of them have great modern electronic background music, better than some night clubs I have been in. Hip Hop in particular has made a noticeable impact on clothes styles, and most big chain stores now have sections which are clearly hip hop street culture styled. I recall in our first year in Dalian, wandering round a big shopping mall, we came across a hip hop singing talent completion. It was an incongruent sight for us, watching all these young Chinese guys and girls rapping on stage with their baseball caps on backwards, their jeans torn at the knees and their waistband hanging low down at the back almost to their knees, so you could read their underwear brand. Not what we expected of China, but it was great fun.

Fortunately, buying shoes was not a problem for me, as I have relatively small feet for my height, so I had no problem buying shoes anywhere in China. Julie on the other hand struggled terribly. Julie was teased constantly by all the wonderful boots and shoes in the shops, with great new styles not seen in the West, but whenever she tried any on, they were all too narrow for her Western foot. So she could only generally buy shoes when she travelled outside of China.

Julie also struggled in the same way as me with buying clothes in the shops, but she found a solution. Instead of buying off the peg, she would get everything made to measure for herself. Within walking distance of our apartment was a large, well known indoor market that specialised in making clothes. People referred to it by the place name, èrqi guǎngchǎng (which means plaza 27). The wives would simply call it Erqi, or Archie. Julie regularly went there with groups of friends on a designer clothing shopping spree, getting amazing dresses and jackets made, at a fraction of the price of the high end equivalent shops. A real life saver for her and her friends. What better girly day out than to have some fun choosing fabrics, agreeing designs and trying on clothes?

Over our six years in Dalian, you could see more and more influence on street fashion coming from the bigger cities and from Japan and Korea. None more so than with people's hair fashions, and particularly for the guys. Some of the hair styles on the younger men became increasingly quite bizarre over time. I grew up in the days of punk and new wave and so I've sported a few weird hairdos in my time, but these new styles are like nothing I've seen before, with exaggerated comb-overs and huge distorted swooshes that seem to be heading towards a comic book, anime style.

Browsing in some of the fashion shops can be disconcerting if you're used to a British shopping experience. The shop assistants follow you round like horny dogs. They do actively try to be helpful by bringing you clothes to look at that you might like, so I can see they are being proactive in their job, so full marks to them. But it just isn't the way British people shop, we like to be left alone to browse, and then have a store assistant around if we need help. I know it's all my own fault for being culturally uncomfortable and anal with all this, but by them continuously bringing stuff up to me it has the opposite effect than what they intend and just makes me want to leave the shop. Another example of how cultures clash.

One of the most striking challenges foreigners discover immediately with Chinese shopping culture is the need to barter in markets. If you find yourself buying anything in a market, from fruit and vegetables to clothes or housewares, you will be expected to barter. The stall keeper will naturally start at a high price, and just because you are an ignorant, 'out of towner' lǎowài, they will inflate this price extremely high. How much you can knock them down varies from city to city and region to region. At the extreme end, if you're after a knock off handbag or fake watch in one of the big tourist traps in Shanghai or Beijing, you can expect to be able to barter them down to 20 or even 10% of the price they first ask. But if you're purchasing more mundane, everyday things in smaller cities, expect to get no more than 30% off. In Dalian, bartering could typically get you maybe 40% off the asking price. But ultimately, if you want the best price for anything, you need to take a Chinese friend with you. That way the shop keeper won't try so hard to rip you off. Throwing a few Chinese words at him also helps to show that you are not so naïve in China as he thinks, but not to the same extent.

But what starts as a bit of harmless touristy fun at the start of your trip to China, really begins to wear you down when you have to barter every time you go to buy basic stuff. After a few months of having to barter for your apples every time at the market, you just start to think what's the point? You're just saving a few cents for having to go through all the pain and hassle of all this lengthy rigmarole. So for basic stuff, I eventually just gave up and paid what they asked. By then I knew what a reasonable price was, so I knew if they were trying to rip me off, and if you become a regular customer then they treat you differently anyway. But where you really need to keep up and sharpen your bartering skills is if you head to the 'fake' market.

China is famous for its 'Knock Offs'. It is part of every tourist experience to wander round the local fake market, try and do some bartering and return home with a bargain 'Gucci' hand bag or two. Hand bags and watches, are the most well-known of the designer fakes, but almost everything is up for grabs in the world of the underground knock off market. Fake designer goods in general, ties, scarves, clothing, fake branded sportswear, and phoney perfumes are the mainstay of every dodgy back street market. Some of these items are certainly produced with low quality materials in seedy back street sweat shops, but some are essentially the real McCoy, pilfered from over extended production runs at the brand's sub-contract factory in China.

I'm not a great fan of cheap knock offs. I understand the novelty and fun of your first one or two visits to the fake market to bag a bargain, but after that I found it all got a bit boring. Though I'm certainly very happy with Julie still preferring to go to the occasional market to expand her considerable designer bag collection rather than head to the official store. Though Dalian in particular is not the place to buy designer goods, as it has a 30% luxury goods tax, inflating prices even more than the rest of China. Dalian, like every major Chinese city, has its fair share of designer shopping malls, with more opening every year. As we lived in the heart of the CBD, there were two very posh designer shopping malls right down the street from us, Times Square and the Galleria. I remember accompanying Julie into our nearby Chanel store during an afternoon of strolling around and retail therapy. There was one particular handbag that Julie fell for. The price was over 4000 US dollars. She 'umed and ahed' over it, but ultimately walked away without it. It's certainly a price that most of us have to think carefully about. Later that year, we found ourselves on vacation in Kota Kinabalu in Malaysian Borneo and we were strolling through the local shopping mall there and low and behold, in the Chanel store there, they had exactly the same handbag, but it was priced at only 1000 US dollars. It just goes to show the effect of pricing for different markets. Travelling internationally so often does open up your eyes to these things, and you slowly work out the best places in the world to get the best deals on things as you're passing through.

Julie tells me she can spot a fake handbag. She says the best way to tell is to look at the zips and the lining inside. Whilst the outside of the bag may look good, you can easily see the difference in quality of these items between the fake and real items. But you have to be careful travelling overseas with any goods like this. In Japan, they clamp down hard on such things, and when you go through customs, if they suspect that you're carrying a fake designer handbag and you can't prove it, they will take a knife and slash it through. Tough if you spent 4000 US dollars on it and don't have the receipt.

One episode in Beijing summed up the whole fake goods and rip off tourist China for me. We were in Beijing on a week's sightseeing, strolling around the tourist shops near Houhai Lake, just north of the Forbidden City, right in the tourist heart of the city. We browsed in this quite large store full of arty Chinese items, paintings, sculptures, etc. Our eye was taken by a table top room divider painted with pretty Chinese artwork. We enquired about the price, the girl behind the counter said 600RMB. We said no thanks, so she dropped it to 550RMB, then down to 500RMB after we again said no. We wandered off round the rest of the store. The same girl came up to us a couple more times with lower offers, and each time we said no. By the time we left the store the price had dropped to 100RMB, a huge reduction from her original offer. The item was quite nice but the whole pushy tone of the hard sell had turned us off to buying it. We thought that was the end of it but no, even as we were walking down the street, the same girl left the shop and chased us down, waving the thing at us and dropping her price even further; 50RMB, 30RMB, and she eventually came down to 10 RMB. That's less than 2% of the original price she offered us, 2%!!! How crazy is that. We still didn't buy it because by dropping the price that low it just revealed to us what a tacky piece of crap it actually was. If they could sell it for 10RMB and still make a profit, what value really is it? And we all know we are going to being ripped off by the original offer price, that's just part of the game, but to be offered 600RMB on an item that the bartering revealed probably cost less than 6 RMB is just an insult to anyone's intelligence.

But the whole fake goods market in China goes well beyond the street markets and pervades every part of the society. Fake French and Australian wines with well-known branded labels on them are for sale in many shops and served in many restaurants. Fake liquor and spirits are commonplace in many bars and hotels, with dangerous levels of methanol added. And the boldness of some of these dodgy characters has to be admired. I have been in a fake Apple store, several rip off Starbucks cafes and the most audacious for me, I have even heard about a whole knock-off Ikea store, those places are huge. How much balls do you have to have to set up a whole giant department store, how well connected do you need to be with the local government and police to pull that off? You have to feel a little admiration for some of these guys. With that much energy and commitment, what could they achieve in the 'legal' world?

CHAPTER 5

THE DELICIOUS FUN OF KILLING FISH IN THE RAIN (OR MY STRUGGLES WITH THE CHINESE LANGUAGE)

Let's start by being honest, the Chinese language is challenging, very challenging. For a Westerner, Chinese might as well be an alien language. If you have grown up immersed in Romanised languages, then there is just no way in, no entry point for you to even begin. At least if you're an English speaker and you look at things written in French or German or Spanish, the letters are familiar and so you have a starting point. But with a pictorial language like Chinese, there is no way in at all. You absolutely need a teacher to hold your hand and guide you through. My journey through the Chinese language started a few months after we arrived. I was really motivated to have a go, even though languages aren't my strongest skill. I was committed to at least 3 years here, so might as well dive in.

The official Chinese language is Mandarin, spoken mainly across the North of the country, but made the official language by the government in the 1950s in order to unify the nation. Today around 70% of Chinese are native speakers of Mandarin, making it the most spoken language on the planet. The Chinese call their language pŭtōnghuà, which means common speech, or Hànyŭ, which means language of the Han. The Han are the main ethnic group in China, accounting for over 90% of the population. The other main language you will hear when travelling to the south of the country is Cantonese, spoken in Hong Kong, Macau and around the Guangzhou region, with around 5% of the country being native speakers. As an international traveller you will inevitably travel through Shanghai at some point, where you will get to hear their unique local Shanghainese language. In reality, there are plenty of other regional languages and many more regional dialects used around the country. The first couple of years of trying to learn Chinese was a frustrating experience as I frequently travelled around the country on business, so got very little consistency in terms of languages and accents to practice with. I thought I was just bad at the language. Eventually, my Chinese friends and colleagues admitted to me that they had the same problem, when they travelled to other parts of their own country, they would have no clue what people were saying, and they were native Mandarin speakers. So after that, I didn't feel so stupid. Mandarin is also widely spoken in other countries in South East Asia, including Singapore, where it is one of their four official languages, and Malaysia. But friends from these regions have told me that they often struggle to get understood in Mainland China because their accents are just so different, even though they are ostensibly speaking the same language.

The official written language is called 'simplified Chinese'. There is also a 'traditional Chinese' form of characters, which are used throughout Hong Kong, Macau and Taiwan, which has more complex character forms. But if you know the simplified characters, I found that the traditional characters can be deciphered pretty easily. The best thing about the written simplified Chinese language is that it is used widely across the whole of the country. All the myriad of confusing dialects and accents that can make learning the spoken language so challenging are not there in the written form. So even if a local pronounces a word differently to what I have learnt, they all write it in the same way. All the different spoken languages use the same simplified Chinese character set, and that's what motivated me so much to learn the characters, not just attempt the spoken aspect of the language.

Many expats have a go at learning Chinese, but given that most are only there on 2 or 3 year contracts, and they have a time consuming day job of course, then most only end up learning a bit of the spoken language. It is the minority that choose to dive into the characters. Whatever path you choose also depends on how your brain is wired, I have a musical background, and an analytical job, and so I guess my brain could process much more easily the subtle sound of the tones and the visual form of the written characters than others students, whilst I struggled with other aspects of the language that others excelled at. Different people have different strengths and so their learning experience is different. I decided early on in my studies that I was going to restrict my learning to speaking, reading and typing only. I deliberately decided not to try to learn to hand write Chinese characters. I just thought it would be a waste of time because how often do any of us even hand write English these days? We spend most of our time typing into our smartphones and into our laptops, so I just decided to focus on building those same skills in Chinese. So to this day, even though I can type Chinese characters and read printed Chinese, I cannot hand write anything, and just as deciphering hand written notes in English can be tough from people with bad handwriting, so in Chinese, hand written notes just look like complete scrawl to me.

What I discovered over the first few months is that learning Chinese is like learning several languages all at the same time. You have to learn pinyin (see later), you have to learn how to use the tones, you have to learn how to say the Chinese words and you have to learn the characters themselves. But there is a positive side to all this, whilst Chinese challenges you with brand new linguistic concepts like tones and pictographic characters, it more than compensates with the simplicity of its grammar. Word order is different to English and other languages, for sure, but easy enough to learn. But get this, there are no verb tenses, so you don't have to learn all those endless lists of conjugated verbs for past, present and future (I am, you are, he is,..., I was, you were, he was,..., etc.) that make English and other Latin based languages so difficult. So no 'past participles' or 'future perfect' tenses! Tense is achieved by adding simple time related adverbs into a sentence. And it gets simpler. There are also no plurals, so you don't need to learn plural versions of all the nouns. Plurals are achieved either by adding numbers or using special measure words related to the type of noun in a sentence.

Pinyin is a written form of Chinese that uses Romanised letters, like English, developed in the 1950s, to help teach the sounds of the words and the correct use of tones. It was developed because Chinese characters are drawn in such a way that they give you no clue as to how to pronounce the word or what tone to use, so you have to learn all that separately parrot fashion. Pinyin is used in all Chinese schools now to teach the foundation of the language. Back in the West, people often ask me how do you type in Chinese, given that all keyboards use Romanised letters? Pinyin is one easy method.

Your first lessons are all about getting your mouth around the classic tones of the language that all foreigners are wary of. Mandarin has four standard active tones, which are captured in pinyin as ā, ǎ, á, à, plus a fifth neutral tone. These tones denote the rising, falling and other variants of the pitch as you pronounce the word. As this is a completely alien concept to Westerners, in order to try to ingrain this into their heads, foreign students usually resort to waving their finger in the air as they try to pronoun the right tone, waving it up, down or whatever, to try to match the tone, in an effort to hard wire the sounds and mouth shapes into their brains. Eventually people don't realise they are even doing it, and so it quickly becomes the only language where you see people conducting along to it with their hands on the street. You will need to go through many training exercises to attune your ear and adjust your tongue to the four tones before you can distinguish them apart. But the tones are crucial, there is no getting around them. Without them, words in Chinese have no meaning. They are as vital a part of creating a word in Chinese as the letters are in an English word.

The challenge for Westerners is that in English we use tones for emphasis, not for meaning, and so it is too easy to think that a Chinese person will get the gist of what you are saying even if you get the tones wrong, not so. Take the simple phrase 'it's raining', one of the first phrases you will try to learn. In Chinese this is 'xià yǔ le'. I had heard a few people saying this simple phrase and learnt it off my colleagues, so in an effort to impress my Chinese teacher, I tried to say this. But instead it came out as 'shā yú le'. She just looked at me with a puzzled look on her face and said, 'What? You are killing fish?' That's what Chinese is like without the correct tones. Be warned, you will make a dick of yourself on many occasions. Another thing I learnt early on is that you have to take care with sentences that have the words 'da' and 'bien' next to each other (and these are very common words), because 'dàbiàn' means to take a shit. There are plenty of other words and pronunciations to watch out for, and you will put your foot in it frequently early on, but just have a good laugh about it, because making mistakes is how you will learn. Though it doesn't help when one of the most difficult words for foreigners to get their tongue around is the most common word you will need, thank you (xièxie). I hear so many different versions of this from foreigners (qiqi, xixi, chercher, sheshe), with most of them sounding like the name of a Panda in a zoo.

All these word and tone combinations look completely different from each other in the written form, as they use completely different characters, but are some of the classic faux pas that Westerners struggle with when trying to comprehend and speak Chinese, as they sound so similar to the untrained ear. However, they all sound completely different from each other to a native Chinese speaker of course, so it can get very frustrating. One such example is the Chinese word for Coke, kělè, which in Chinese literally means amusing or entertaining, but is also a very cunning phonetic word play on the Chinese word for thirsty, which is kělè, pretty clever huh? The coke/thirsty thing was one of my earliest frustrations. In writing they are easily distinguishable as the characters are very different, but to me the words kělè, and kele (note the subtle change of accent on the last 'e') sounded exactly the same, whilst to my Chinese friends, none of them had ever considered that these two words might sound similar until I asked them about it. To them, these were two completely different words that they could never mix up.

The full name for Coca Cola in Chinese is kěkǒu kělè, which brings two words together that literally mean 'delicious fun', and is a great example of Western-Chinese cross-over branding. The marketing department earned their money that day! It is an example of what is called a loanword, a phonetic version of a foreign word that is easier for Chinese to say, and there are lots of them in Chinese. These include simple everyday words like bāshì (bus), kāfēi (coffee), péigēn (bacon), běibí (baby), international place names, like Lúndūn (London), Bālí (Paris), Duōlúnduō (Toronto), and more specialist loanwords like mǎlāsōng (marathon), bāzǔkǎ (bazooka), pánníxīlín (penicillin). But some of them can get increasingly unrecognisable as phonetic versions of English words, like Màidāngláo (McDonalds) or sānmíngzhì (sandwich), until you understand how the Chinese language works and the kind of sounds that Chinese people are used to getting their mouths around.

And just like all languages, there are peculiar idiosyncrasies and similar words that even the Chinese get wrong. The classic one is jiǔdiàn (hotel), and jiǔdiǎn (9 o'clock). I have sat in a car with two Chinese people while they tried to agree a time to pick a visiting colleague up from their hotel and got very confused. But just like with any potential confusion of meaning, you will just need to understand the context of the sentence to know what is being said. I had one colleague with the name Ben Tang. He was an American from California, but with Chinese heritage. The Chinese thought it has highly amusing when he arrived, as Ben Tang in China means 'idiot' (bèndàn).

And as you get deeper into the language, you start to learn that some things that sound so exotic to a foreigner are in reality just everyday mundane things just like back home. When I meet people with exotic names like Mr Huang and Mr Bai, the reality is that these are just the Chinese words for Mr Yellow and Mr White!

But I can't keep pretending that everything is the fault of the 'confusing' Chinese language that caused me to stumble on my path of learning the language. Sometimes I was just plain dumb and used the wrong word. I was in a coffee shop in Shanghai, ordering my kāfēi nátiě (coffee latte). My drink arrived, and I'd given the guy a 100RMB note. I waited for my change, and I waited, and I waited. Eventually I said to the guy in my finest Chinese, 'méiyou lǐngdài, méiyou lǐngdài'. He just looked at me with a blank impression. I pulled out some money and waved it at him 'méiyou lǐngdài'. He eventually understood and I got my change and walked off. I walked away with my take away coffee and my change feeling pretty smug that my Chinese lessons were finally paying off. It was only much later that it dawned on me that instead of telling the guy I was waiting for my change, I actually told him that 'I wasn't wearing a tie.'

The mistakes work both ways with the language of course and on any trip to China you are always guaranteed to see some amusing misuse of the English language on signs and emblazoned on people's clothing when walking around the city. Gathering great examples of Chinglish can become quite an obsession for some expats. You just get to see it so often and in the most unexpected of places. Walking around any city centre is always a great source of Chinglish fun. I once nearly peed my pants at a sign in a shopping mall which listed 'Fuck Goods' (this should have read 'dry goods', but the word for dry in Chinese is gan which is also used as a slang word for fuck). You can see how some of these mistranslations have arisen because someone has just gone to a Chinese-English dictionary and taken the first word on the list, but we all know languages can be much more subtle than that. It is hard to understand why people just don't check these things before going ahead with making a sign, or printing a T-shirt. Though I am sure there are plenty of signs in the West designed for Chinese tourists that are equally hilarious to them and just as collectable, there's probably a website somewhere called Englinese. Another great sign I saw in a store was 'Shoplifters will be Prostituted'. In parks you will sometimes see signs saying 'No pissing or shitting on the grass', and I've seen variants of this next to bus stops. If you're lucky, you might also get to see the infamous coffee shop rip off 'Star Fucks'.

Restaurant menus are another classic source of Chinglish mishaps. One local Japanese restaurant we frequented in Dalian, had listed on the English version of their menu 'deep fired cock', but this of course was simply fried chicken. The further out you venture from the more modern civilised cities and out into the sticks of China, the more extreme, surreal and plain wrong the English translations become. At a smaller city on the outskirts of Dalian, near where we built the factory, the local hotel we often used proudly displayed on its menu 'Wing miscellaneous bacteria pot', which appeared to be some kind of soup, and 'Stewed opium fish', which I never tried myself but I heard it was quite popular.

Public Toilets are always a great source of amusing Chinglish signs, displaying stick man signs like 'do not squat on the toilet seat'. Every time I go back to China, there are more and more safety and prohibition signs in public toilets. At the last count there were six different signs on the back of my toilet cubicle door in Shanghai Pudong airport, explaining 'don't do this, don't do that'. Very soon there will be more sign than door.

People watching also throws up many Chinglish opportunities, as there are always plenty of 'exotic' English words and phrases strewn across T-shirts and over other clothing. We do exactly the same in the West, putting exotic Chinese and Japanese characters and national flags on clothing makes it seem somehow more glamorous. It's exactly the same in China, just the other way around. But of course in China, they don't always get it quite right. Firstly there are the T-shirts with completely random English words printed on them, like 'London artichoke dream' or 'apple happiness crown', and then there are the particularly memorable attempts at cool phrases I saw which read 'Fart Sexy Style' and 'Don't fu*k my ass'. Walking down the street in China can be a constant source of amusement watching out for classic howlers like these. In one major high street baseball cap store, I swear I saw a baseball cap with the worlds 'Jesus Fucks' proudly printed across the top. You also see Chinese distortions of global advertising slogans on T-shirts, such as 'Just Fuck It', or just plainly mis-spelt knock off band T-shirts, like Linken Park, or Nervana.

However frustrating learning the Chinese language has been for me over the years, and there have been many times when I thought that despite all my hard work I wasn't progressing or worse, even going backwards, I have ultimately thoroughly enjoyed the challenge. As I said in Chapter 1, my best everyday street teachers were my two drivers, Huang and Fang. But when I comes to formal teachers, I have had three or four in the five and a half years I was studying Chinese in the country. The longest serving and most patient of my teachers was Summer, who stood by me for the last 4 years of our time in Dalian. During the last couple of years, my language abilities were sufficient such that we spent many, many hours together chatting in Chinese about all sorts of subjects during my lessons. Summer developed my language skills to the point of being able to sit formal advanced qualifications. It was never my intention to sit any exams whilst I was learning the language but then we had only signed up for a 3 year contract, and we did not know we were going to stay in the country for so much longer. But eventually, after 4 years of learning, Julie said to me, 'why don't you take an exam? It would be great to have a formal qualification to show for all your hard work over the years'. I couldn't really disagree with her, so why not? But what exam? It turned out that there is a formal system of Chinese language qualifications for foreigners learning Chinese in the country, called HSK, or Hànyǔ Shuǐpíng Kǎoshì, which means Chinese Language Proficiency Test.

To pass HSK Level 1, students are required to start by learning 100 of the most simple Chinese words and phrases. HSK 2 adds another 200 words and phrases on top of this, at which stage students will have a good grasp of basic Chinese and be able to communicate on simple everyday tasks. HSK 3 adds a further 300 words, so to pass, a student would need to be able to communicate in Chinese at a reasonable level in their daily lives. Level 4 adds another 600 words on top, so to pass this exam, a student would need to be proficient with the use of 1200 everyday words and phrases, which means they are able to talk with Chinese people on a wide range of topics and start to attempt reading a newspaper. Having a qualification at HSK Level 4 is a basic requirement to be able to take a job in a Chinese company. Beyond this, HSK 5 adds another

1200 words to the student's vocabulary, meaning that they would be able to use and understand around 2500 words in total, taking them essentially to street level fluency in the language. HSK 6 increases the overall vocabulary to over 5000 words, up to the level of academic Chinese proficiency.

When it comes to the exams, from HSK 3 onwards, there is no pinyin in the test, so everything is done in Chinese characters only, and this is what challenges most foreign learners, because they tend to hang on to their familiar Romanised lettering system as long as possible. As I had already been learning the language for four and a half years, my teacher put me straight in for the HSK 3 exam, which I passed no problem. In fact, by far the hardest thing about sitting the HSK 3 exam was not the Chinese, it was the 'sitting the exam' part. I had not sat a formal exam for more than 30 years, since my University days. It was a very weird feeling driving to the local University, where the exam was being held, and having to find the examination room, armed with my enrolment details. With so many young people in the country, Chinese universities tend to be very big establishments, and so finding the right building and the right floor was already a challenge. But once there, I went in and sat down and immediately started feeling pretty lonely. I was the only one there. In the whole of Dalian, a city of almost 7 million people, was I the only foreigner taking the test? The exams were held once a month, but still, I expected more than just me. Eventually another European guy turned up and then a Japanese girl. So just the three of us. So I was sat at the desk with the test computer in front of me and the invigilator came in and barked out all these instructions in Chinese and away we went. I was sitting my first exam in over 30 years, very strange and very tense.

The Chinese questions were okay for me, but the biggest challenge was the time that was counting down in the corner of the screen. All the questions were timed and you really did not have long to answer them, no thinking time, you just had to go with your gut, so the time pressure was enormous, and on top of that the room had a big clock straight in front of me ticking off the 90 minutes of my ordeal. But I got through it of course. A couple of weeks later my results came through and I had passed with flying colours and could start feeling proud of myself. I started working towards HSK 4 almost immediately, worked hard over the next year and got close to sitting that exam, but our circumstances changed quickly at that point, my contract came to an end and we had to leave the country, so I never got to sit the HSK 4 exam even though I had done all the work. Still, I had all the knowledge in my head and used it pretty often in my daily life.

It had always been an intended milestone of mine to get proficient enough in the Chinese language that I could stand up and give a speech in front of Chinese people. Never one to shy away from a challenge, I tried this out a few times, even in my early years in China and did okay. I am always of the opinion that the best way to learn to do something is just to dive in with both feet and do your best. I spoke in front of colleagues at a couple of meetings and conferences, I even spoke in front of a huge room full of Chinese students at one of the Shanghai universities. All just for a few minutes and just simple stuff, but it was a start. I never got any heckling and I didn't notice any blank faces, so I think I got understood well enough. But all this was leading up to my ultimate speech. When we finally left Dalian, it had always been my plan to be able to stand up and deliver my farewell speech in Chinese, and this is exactly what I did. I felt very proud that I had developed enough as a person and as a Chinese speaker to the level that I could deliver an important speech off the cuff. It was a difficult moment, but one I had thought hard about for a long time.

CHAPTER 6

NUCLEAR FROG
(OR A TASTE OF CHINA)

One of the great joys of travelling to foreign climes is experiencing all the different food that new countries and cultures have to offer. Food is certainly always right at the heart of any China experience. Forget what you know from your Chinese restaurant experience back home. When you're in China, the sights, smells and tastes can blow you away. Now that can sometimes be good, and sometimes be bad, but when it comes to meal time in China, it is certainly never going to be dull.

In China, they claim there are 8 classic Chinese cuisines. These are Sichuan (the ultra-hot chilli laden dishes from the far West of China), Hunan (equally spicy, but with a hot and sour twist), Cantonese (the most well known in the West, tends to be a little sweet), Fujian (lighter and more subtle in flavour, with sweet and sour tones), Zhejiang (simple fresh food with a mellow taste), Anhui (a hearty peasant style food, reflecting this mountainous region), Jiangsu (sweet, sticky and very colourful dishes, the ultimate banquet food), and Shandong (seafood and noodles, with lots of vinegar and salt). Our home in Dalian is very much part of the Shandong cuisine region and is very well known by Chinese as the ultimate 'Seafood City'. Not surprising since it's surrounded on three sides by the sea. There are seafood restaurants everywhere in the city, with names like Fisherman's Wharf and Harbour City.

Apart from some of the food itself, the whole business of eating it can be quite a challenge in China. Many Westerners struggle with chopsticks and some just never get the hang of them. I personally have never had any problem, and have been using them since I was a teenager back home in England. But the Chinese take their chopstick skills to a whole other level. On one of my business trips to China, before we moved there to live, I recall sitting in the hotel restaurant at breakfast and watching some guy picking up and eating a fried egg with chopsticks. I was just amazed, how is that even possible? Well, a couple of years after moving to China, I was doing the same thing. Julie had not really tried chopsticks before moving to China, but no fear, she took to them like a Beijing duck to soy sauce. Julie is ambidextrous, and so is really great at manual dexterity tasks, hence chopsticks proved no problem for her. The main difficulty she has is deciding which hand to use. Her skills grew to the point that she was stopped at a shopping mall event a couple of years ago to try out some of the World record attempts they had set up for shoppers to try their hand at. She was challenged to see how many peanuts she could pick up in one minute using chopsticks and place in a bowl. She was only one off the world record, and that all left handed. She drew quite a crowd that day. One of the mildly racist things we have to put up with as foreigners living in China, is the amount of times you sit in a restaurant, at the same dinner table as your Chinese friends, and the waiting staff bring a knife and fork for you, no one else, and plonk it in front of you. Pretty annoying when you have spent so long perfecting your chopstick skills.

Another thing I found pretty hard to get used to at first was just how early the Chinese have dinner. And subsequently just how early it is all over. If you go to dinner with friends in China, you are basically eating at 6pm or earlier, and after all the great food, great conversation and plenty of drinking, by 8pm it is all over. At first I was quite stunned by how quickly the evening all grinds to a halt. One minute you're all laughing and joking and the next minute someone has paid the bill and everyone's up off their chairs to go home. In the West, it not unusual to be starting the meal at this time, so it was tough to get used to. But you have to go with the flow. It eventually became pretty routine for me with business visitors to go straight from work to the restaurant and dive straight into the festivities. But I learnt to appreciate that this actually may be a better way of doing things.

In the West it is usual to take your visitors back to their hotel after work so they can freshen up and then pick them up later in the evening to go to dinner. But this basically takes up your entire evening, as you have to travel to and from home, or worst still, sit around their hotel waiting if your home is too far away. And dinner can end 11pm or later sometimes. At least with the Chinese timing, everything is over by 8pm and you can go home and relax and recover, and get some sleep. Even if you all take the drinking on to a bar or karaoke after dinner, you can all still be finished by 10pm, giving plenty of time to get home and sleep it all off, ready to start work again in the morning. So in the end, after much practice, I found it to be a much superior way of timing your business entertainment. Another valuable lesson that China has taught me!

Formal and business dinners in China are normally really grand occasions, held in opulent private rooms, with sumptuous gold and red décor and huge round lazy Susan tables, accommodating 20 or more people round each of them. I've been lucky enough to enjoy such occasions many times with business colleagues, customers, business partners, government officials and at wedding parties. They all usually follow a pretty similar agenda, regardless of the particular type of occasion, with a beer, or tea, and small talk as everyone arrives, then the guest of honour is seated in the chair opposite the main door, and everyone else sits down. Once seated, all the starter dishes begin to come out. In the West we are generally used to having our food delivered individually on plates just for us in the standard order of starter, main course, dessert. Forget this in China, the vast majority of dishes turn up as and when they arrive from the kitchen, in whatever order they arrive, and are placed in the centre of the lazy Susan as communal dishes for everyone to pick at. They do follow the same loose order of starter, main course, dessert, but there are usually so many different and strange dishes coming out that it is often difficult to tell which is meant to be which and where one course has ended and another begun. By the end of the meal, the table will be littered with the leftovers of all the different courses, so it all merges into one. Despite the variety and sumptuousness of the main dishes, the end of the meal is usually rounded off very simply with some watermelon, and sometimes other fruits, as a palate cleanser. Of the mains, there will usually be one of two centre piece dishes that arrive for some wow factor, like a sheep's head or a sweet and sour mandarin fish, all very dramatically presented, though often with minimal stuff you can actually eat off it. At the end of the banquet it is quite normal for doggy bags to be prepared as there will always be so much left over. The show of wealth that is part of the culture of hosting a meal means that there is always far too much food brought out, with all the inevitable waste that follows.

Grand banquet food is almost always Shanghai/Jiangsu style cuisine, no matter where in the country it is served. This style of food is very sweet and always very colourful. The starters are generally cold and personally I find them a bit sickly, slimy and unappetising and just wait for the main courses. Once the hot dishes come out, they are usually delicious, and you will normally see the closest things to what passes for Chinese food back in the West brought out, like sweet and sour pork. You will never go hungry at these banquets, as there is so much food both in quantity and variety that even the most challenged foreigners will find something familiar to eat, even if it's just the steamed rice at the end of the meal. Rice is always a separate dish and the timing of when it appears in the meal varies from region to region. Some regions have it first, before the main dishes arrive, some areas don't have it at all unless you order it specifically. But these banquets come at a price and that price is the huge quantities of alcohol you will be drinking. The next chapter expands more on the drinking culture in China, and specifically how it is woven into the banqueting process.

Of all the different types of Chinese cuisine, one of my favourites, and often the favourite of many Westerners, is Sichuan. These dishes always come smothered in masses of red chillies, to the extent that it's sometimes difficult to tell whether you have eaten all the food because the dishes look exactly the same after you've finished eating them, a pile of superhot red chilies which are still there. There are plenty of Sichuan restaurants to be found around every city and Dalian was no exception. We discovered a great one early on in our time there, called Mala 100%. We found out that it was part of a restaurant chain and that málà means 'spicy and numbing', referring to the fact that the food is so hot that it numbs your mouth. Apart from all the chillies, they also use a lot of whole peppercorns in the cooking, and there was no better example of ultra-hot Sichuan cooking on their menu than spicy bullfrog. This was a dish we discovered on our very first visit there, and which became a must to order every time we returned, which was quite often. Spicy bullfrog comes swimming in hot chilli oil, with loads of hot and whole chillies floating on it and seasoned further with whole sprigs of peppercorns, still on the bush, dangling in the broth. An absolute mouth numbing experience that we soon rechristened as 'Nuclear Frog'. It was one of those infamous dishes where you always suffered the next day for it, but couldn't wait to go back for more punishment, the culinary equivalent of S&M. Mala 100% became a go to venue for our expat friends for two or three years. Another first at Mala 100% for us was the 'towers of beer' that they sold, large clear plastic cylinders with a tap at the bottom. They held 3 litres each and were perfect for keeping a thirsty group supplied with much needed cooling ale, and fitted great on a lazy Susan. A not so great discovery at this place was the 'blueberry health beer' they advertised. Something you had to try once just for the novelty factor, but in my opinion, it wasn't beer and I'm sure it wasn't healthy.

Any tourist trip to Beijing would not be complete without a stroll down Donghuamen tourist street, in Wangfujing district. This is pretty close to Tiananmen Square and is lined with a seemingly unending row of food stalls. Open during the day, but particularly busy and vibrant in the evening, this is a food market designed to give visitors an unforgettable Chinese experience, by resorting to foodie shock tactics. Not a place for the fainthearted, but if you're looking for a truly unique and memorable experience you will not be disappointed by the huge range of the most extreme foods imaginable for sale; star fish, tarantulas, baby sharks, scorpions, deep fried crickets, large beetles, silk worms, huge centipedes, skinned snakes, stinky tofu, fried tripe, chicken hearts, lamb testicles, and many other bizarre and unusual things, all skewered on a stick. They even have goat's penis wound around a skewer, fresh for the barbeque, plus a range of other animal members to choose from. It's a smelly, noisy, steamy, crowded place that challenges you on many levels, but it's so vibrant, colourful, interesting and fun, and guaranteed to give you a great travel story for the future.

The whole thing is laid on just for the tourists, Chinese people don't really eat these things. The only people you actually see eating star fish and scorpions are backpackers looking for an extreme selfie of themselves munching on a star fish arm or a scorpion claw, to put on their Instagram page. There are also plenty of more 'normal' Chinese snacks for sale if you do get hungry, such as dumplings, spring rolls, and sugar coated fruits. If you're after more substantial Chinese food, then there are plenty of other food street markets open in the area, selling what you would consider proper Chinese dishes, very popular in the evening and always an invigorating source of evening entertainment, even though they're largely populated by tourists.

Beyond the tourist traps of Beijing, out in real China, whilst they don't actually eat the kind of nonsense that the tourist food market displays skewered on a stick, you will find real people eating things which you will find very strange and that will challenge the boundaries of what you consider as food. In six years living in and travelling around China, I have had so many things dumped on the dinner table in front of me that surprised and shocked me, some I expected to encounter, and some that were a complete surprise. But you expect to be confronted with strange things to eat in China and right across Asia, this is part of the whole joy of travelling and of experiencing new things.

The first and most well-known of the weirder side of the food that people associate with China is chicken feet. Everyone knows Chinese people eat chicken feet, so you know at some point living in China you are going to be confronted with them at dinner. The Chinese don't actually call them chicken feet, once prepared and served at the table, in the Chinese language they call them 'Phoenix Claw', which makes them sound much more exotic and palatable. I tried these things a few times in my first couple of years in an attempt to wean myself onto a few Chinese delicacies, but I just couldn't get the hang of them. After plenty of nibbling on what is essentially a bit of hard rubbery gristle, I eventually gave up. I decided that whether phoenix claw or chicken feet, these things just aren't food and I don't see the point in eating them. Chicken feet are just skin, bones, and tendons, but no muscle, so there is no 'meat' on them. They taste of nothing and the texture is not very pleasant, so what's the point? There are usually dozens of other things on the table that are really tasty, so why waste your dinner time eating something so bland? So why do the Chinese eat them? Like with many of the more weird foods, there is a long held belief that they are very healthy and good for you. Chicken feet are packed with protein, minerals, collagen and cartilage that are supposed to be easily absorbed by the body, and are considered to deliver benefits for your joints, skin and contribute to a healthy heart. As with most of these types of claims, scientific studies are few and far between and so the benefits are not unequivocally proven, but I guess with most of these things it's what you believe that counts.

There is also a school of thought that suggests the reason that the Chinese have developed a culture of eating chicken feet and other strange things that in the West would be thrown away as garbage, goes back to times when famine spread across the country and people were forced to eat anything and everything they could find, including the parts of animals they would normally cut off and throw away. And remarkably, the last widespread famine was only 60 years ago, spread by a combination of natural and political disasters. And I don't raise this with any intent to judge. I am completely sure that if any of us were starving, any one of us would eat an insect to survive.

So you're at a company dinner with all your Chinese colleagues. It's bound to happen one day, the sea cucumber moment! The first time a sea cucumber is placed in front of you on the dinner table, your first thoughts are of an overinflated condom. It's got that synthetic greenish shade to it, it's got some alarming knobbly bits all over and it tastes faintly rubbery (or so my wife tells me). Sea cucumber is another well-known item that is put on the 'strange foods' list by most Westerners, and is another one I have tried to get used to whilst living in China. But unlike chicken feet, I did slowly get used to eating sea cucumber. Don't be fooled by the name, sea cucumber is not a vegetable, it is a marine animal, it just that it is the size and shape of a cucumber and hence the name. It is often served grated and used in or on other dishes to add salty flavour, but that is too easy to consume. The real challenge is in squaring up to a whole one, and that's what I did many times over the years, and came off the winner on most occasions. I find sea cucumber not unpleasant, a little bland, but it is essentially a big wobbly lump of protein, very low in fat, so I can get my logical brain around this as a 'healthy' food, and it definitely goes into this bracket for the Chinese.

Where we lived in Dalian, they had something called the 100 day diet, where you were supposed to eat one sea cucumber every day for 100 days, in an attempt to revitalise your whole body. As the seafood city of China, located in the cold water of the North, Dalian is supposed to have the best sea cucumber and abalone in the whole of China. It is considered a real delicacy and there are shops in Dalian that the only thing they sell is sea cucumber, fresh and dried. Some of these are very high end stores in the middle of the financial district, selling very expensive sea cucumber, so a 100 day diet of the stuff could end up being a very expensive exercise.

The biggest sea cucumber occasions for me have always been at Chinese weddings. Whenever Julie and I have been lucky enough to attend the wedding parties of some of our Chinese friends, one of the dishes brought out on each table is always a huge steaming pile of freshly prepared sea cucumbers. I always tuck in straight away and get my first one out of the way before I dive into the other foods. Partly out of respect, partly to show our Chinese friends that we have integrated into the culture and partly because I feel like I have achieved something by being able to get stuck into real Chinese food. I guess serving this at a wedding is some show of wealth by the bride's parents, considering it is such a delicacy.

Once you've mastered the art of the sea cucumber, you can then move on up (or is that down?) the food chain and try the next weird sea food on the list. Eating spiny sea urchin is a bit like sucking on snot. It has that consistency, and a little of the flavour. But just like eating your own boogers can become addictive, so does eating sea urchin tend to grow on you. For most of us in the West, the only time we see a spiny sea urchin is in the bottom of an aquarium or dried, polished and on display in a shop as a pretty household decoration. So to be confronted with it as a food item for the first time is quite a strange situation to find yourself in. They tend to range between the size of an apple and a grapefruit, and are covered with very long sharp spines. If you've spent any time in China, you will have already gone through the chicken feet and sea cucumber challenges, so you will be less and less shocked by weird foods, so rather than just going 'yuk, I'm not eating that', the first time a spiny sea urchin is placed in front of you, you just think, how am I supposed to eat this? You look around the table of course for some inspiration and some instructions from your fellow dinners, though usually it is brought to your table ready prepared with the top cut off. You look inside and peer in to this yellowish gunge at the bottom. They are served raw (just think of it as sushi or sashimi) and the flesh can be scooped out with a teaspoon. I still don't order them myself at a restaurant (that would be weird), but I always secretly hope someone at the table will because I have now learnt to actually look forward to their slithery salty freshness. All doused with a good helping of soy sauce, squirted in the middle, mixed up to that mucus consistency and then slithering down your throat like choking back your own vomit. Yum yum!

Dalian, and China in general, has plenty of other challenging sea food to tempt the most adventurous of palates. Sea slugs and sea snails are always an experience when they appear at the dinner table. The very first time Julie and I had dinner with our local colleagues during the first week we moved to Dalian, we were confronted with a fist sized sea snail on our plates. A first for me, let alone Julie. As this was a dinner in our honour, when these things appeared, which to some would be the highlight of the dinner and very expensive items, everyone looked to us to start, and nobody would start without the guests of honour tucking in first. We did our best but it was obvious we needed some help. The immediate challenge is getting at the thing. It is hidden deep within a big shell, so you need to try and ease it out with a toothpick. What emerges is a large rubbery creature, just like a large land snail, with a poo sac hanging off it. No need to eat the poo sac, but nobody tells you that of course! Julie has a little nibble on the snail, but ultimately just couldn't handle hers, it was just too extreme for her first week in China. I ate mine but it was like chewing through a rubber tyre, not a particularly pleasant experience or one I have chosen to repeat again since.

Other fishy dinner experiences we have been through include being served shark fin soup, and when we refused to eat it because of the cruelty, we were told off by the hosts because apparently 'it's just a fish'. It is also quite shocking to see the amount of seahorses on sale in shops and markets, both alive and dried, and served in various restaurant dishes. Seahorses are portrayed as cute, friendly things in Western culture, whereas in China they are prized for their supposed medicinal qualities, so it's always going to be one of the 'culture shock' moments when you come across dried seahorses for sale in your local supermarket. We have also seen tiny baby jelly fish in little pots for sale at the seaside, but were never quite sure if you were meant to cook them and eat them or keep them as pets. I remember the first time we were served a salad with shredded jelly fish on top, Julie said she bit her tongue whilst eating it but didn't even realise what she had done because the jelly fish was exactly the same texture and taste as her tongue.

One of the strangest and most memorable marine life experiences I had in Dalian was when I was walking down the road one day, back from a stroll round the harbour and came across a man standing at the side of the road dangling a humongous turtle from a pole that we was holding. He had this thing suspended in mid-air, swinging in the breeze just over the edge of the sidewalk, so that every passing car driver could get a good luck. It was easily two feet long, maybe three. It looked like he had just caught the turtle in the bay. He was obviously hoping to sell it, but just like with the baby jelly fish, I was not quite sure whether this was meant for making turtle soup or to keep as a pet. I guess as long as he got paid for it, he didn't care. I have no idea how much he expected to sell it for. Whilst trade in sea turtles is illegal in many countries, it is not in China, where turtles are still eaten and used in Chinese medicine. You can even buy small turtles at local supermarkets, where you can pick them out live from a tank and watch them get butchered in front of you.

The whole seafood experience in China, and particularly in Dalian, was a never ending eye opener of new and strange creatures. Dalian is littered with seafood restaurants everywhere you go. As soon as you step inside, the first thing you will usually see is the banks of fish tanks, from which you can go and select your live catch of the day for your evening meal. It is always a great experience looking around the variety of things on offer swimming around in the tanks. I have even seen salamanders for sale in some restaurants. As if what I have described so far isn't weird enough, some of the seafood restaurants I went in would also have a second, back room, where they displayed the really bizarre stuff. Stepping in there was liking stepping onto the set of the movie 'Alien'. They would always be dark and humid, and the tanks would be filled with the weirdest looking slithery creatures that you have ever laid eyes on. Things which look like intestines coiled round, marine animals resembling a variety of other internal organs, and organisms which looked very like Alien face huggers slithering up the side of tanks. A very cool experience but not for the nervous or those prone to nightmares.

One of the most infamous, but certainly not back room, seafood delicacies to be found in China, originating from Japan, is 'Fugu', or the notorious 'puffer fish'. We have all seen these amazing creatures, which puff themselves up into a huge ball with all their spines sticking out to protect themselves. They have a very distinctive appearance and are instantly recognisable. But they are also famous for the fact that they are extremely poisonous, so why would anyone attempt to eat them? Several of their internal organs, and particularly the liver, contain a deadly neurotoxin, called tetrodotoxin, which is 1200 times deadlier than cyanide. The poison works by paralyzing the muscles, which means that the victim stays fully conscious, but is unable to breathe, and eventually dies from asphyxiation. There is no known antidote. Dalian has a handful of Fugu restaurants around the city, easily noticeable because they hang a great big plastic puffer fish outside, so there is no mistaking what you are getting yourself into. Chefs need to undergo two to three years training to learn how to prepare the meat to avoid contamination by the poison, in order to obtain a special license and be able to legally prepare the fish, to minimise the high risk of poisoning. The scariest part is that the role of the Fugu chef is not to eliminate the poison altogether from the dish, but to reduce it to the extent that the diner experiences some mild effects of poisoning, producing tingling sensations and euphoria. Fugu is extremely expensive and served raw in thin slices as sashimi. I have eaten Fugu a couple of times in Dalian, always as part of an expensive business dinner. It has a very delicate taste and if you like sashimi, then it's really worth a try. The serving of Fugu is banned altogether in Europe, though there are a handful of licensed restaurants across the US.

Crab is very popular in China and the height of the crab season is around October and November, which is when the famous 'hairy crab' matures. Hairy crabs are fist-sized, with a dark green back, and reddish-golden claws covered in brown fur and much prized for their sweet taste, including their roe. Hairy crab season is very noticeable in China because live crabs appear for sale everywhere and restaurants bring out their special hairy crab menus. You even see crabs for sale in airports during this time. In Shanghai Pudong airport, we saw a whole shop front full of crabs tied up neatly with string for easy transport. At first we thought these were dead, boiled and trussed up ready for sale, but on closer inspection you could see that these mostly dormant creatures displayed the occasional twitch, so they were all still very much alive, though pretty quiet. There were also other types of seafood on sale at the airport, and this is after security, by the departure gates, so people are expected to buy these things and get on an airplane with them. Seems a bit bizarre to me, what if you are connecting to a long international flight? Won't it get a bit stinky in the cabin with fresh seafood packed in someone's luggage? The best hairy crab comes from Yangcheng Lake in Jiangsu Province, and prices can get crazy for the biggest and the best specimens. As this is China, 'fake' hairy crabs inevitably emerge on the market during this period.

Having watched many Chinese people devouring all kinds of seafood over the years, I can see that there is definitely an art and a level of skill to tackling some of these things correctly and efficiently. None more so that when eating crab. Watching some people take a crab apart in a restaurant is quite amazing. The skill they display in dismembering the beast piece by piece and using different parts of the claws and shell to scoop out the flesh from all the nooks and crannies is a real art form. Over about 20 minutes there is absolutely nothing left to eat on the crab. If I tackle a crab I just eat the easy to get to parts, the main body and big claws, I always feel the rest of it is just too much effort, but not these guys.

Any trip to the local supermarket was always very entertaining. Apart from the live turtles and crabs, there are many other live fish and seafood on display. We learnt to walk very quickly past the tank of live razor shells. Hanging vertically in the water, they squirt water out periodically, high into the air, like an organic fountain display. So unsuspecting shoppers often get a good dousing if strolling past at the wrong time. Even the fruit and vegetable display is entertaining, though nothing there that spits water at you, it's all pretty inert (usually). As a Westerner you're used to seeing a wide variety of fruit and vegetables in your local supermarket, even a variety of more exotic things, but even I had never seen some of the foodstuffs considered normal in China. Many of the standard vegetables that are familiar in any Western supermarket have their own Chinese versions, with Chinese broccoli, Chinese asparagus, Thai eggplants, all looking very different to what you see back home. There are also wide Asian varieties of radish on sale that you just never see in the West, much bigger, with different colours, textures and tastes, and Asian versions of cucumbers. There are wonderful Chinese yams, which I love steamed, strange varieties of gourd, like bitter melon, several types of root, including my favourite, lotus root, and the odd Chinese version of mushrooms, back fungus, which take some getting used to at first, but which I absolutely love. Who would have thought a walk round the vegetable aisles would be so eye opening and entertaining?

Another classic food experience in China is eating dog meat, a shocking practice to most in the West, where dogs are domesticated pets. It's well known the world over as a Korean delicacy but also practiced in parts of China. Because of Dalian's location, it has a strong influence from Korea and Japan, and so there are many such restaurants, including a few dog meat places. The restaurant names always include gǒuròu (dog meat) in the title, so there is nothing back street or hidden about this. If you really want to avoid one of these places, then you absolutely need to learn the Chinese character for dog so you don't wander into the 'wrong' restaurant for lunch. There is a dog meat restaurant very close to the airport, I know because I've been there. That's the one and only time I have eaten dog meat. I was invited there by my colleagues one lunch time, so I thought I'd give it a try, why not. The dog meat we had was in a hot pot type stew. It was fine, just kind of stringy and sinuous. Okay, but I would not rush back. I've discussed this practice with colleagues in China and Korea, and they all told me that these days, eating dog meat is considered rather old fashioned, something middle aged men do, not at all popular with younger people.

In China there is growing social pressure from anti dog eating campaigners to try to ban the breeding and sale of dogs for eating. This is particularly targeted at the annual Yulin dog eating festival held every June, in Guangxi province in the South East of the country, where thousands of dogs are slaughtered over the course of the 10 day event. The media around his time is always full of reports of the immense cruelty surrounding the festival, ranging from the inhumane cage conditions, with scores crammed together into very small cages for transport, up to skinning dogs alive and boiling them alive on the street. There is also growing suspicion that many of the dogs that find themselves transported to the festival are pets stolen from other parts of the country. Some of them are a dead giveaway when you see photos of dogs at the festival still with their collars on. But despite all this, the Chinese government has yet to ban the festival, even though it is not a cultural tradition at all, and only started in 2009, as a purely commercial event. However, given the comments I have heard, the eating of dog meat does seems to be a practice that is on the decline and so may one day die out. It's certainly something I will not be doing again.

If the thought of eating dog meat makes your toes curl and your stomach heave, then you haven't heard anything yet. I haven't started yet on the insects. Silkworms are not uncommon to be served up when you dine with Chinese people, certainly not at a grand banquet, but it's not unusual to see them in a normal street restaurant. I have seen them brought out several times over the years. The first time they were brought out, we were at a barbeque restaurant, and someone ordered a plate of silkworm pupae. These basically look like fat maggots, about two centimetres long. At first I thought they were dead and cooked, but as soon as they were placed on the hot plate in the centre of the table, they all started to wake up pretty quickly, all wriggling and popping as they cooked. On a different occasion, someone ordered adult silkworms, which are mature, adult insects about three centimetres long. These were definitely cooked, as they were fried to a hard crispy brown. There were a couple of kids with us at the table and they tucked in with gusto. So I thought, if they can eat them, so can I. I nibbled my way through one or two, and like some of the other strange Chinese foods, I just didn't see what the fuss was about. It didn't really taste of anything. It was sort of mildly crunchy but not particularly pleasant. The worse part of it is that the wings tend to break off in your mouth and stick to the top of you gullet as you try to swallow, making you want to constantly gag. Not nice when you're trying to tease out a bit of leg from between your teeth. Not recommended.

The Chinese dining experience is not just challenging at times from the point of view of the food being served, but also how they serve it can be quite uncomfortable and in some cases downright dangerous. Hot pot restaurants are common across China, and especially in the North. Here, you all sit around a table with a hole in the middle and the waitress brings along a big pan of broth. Once she gets it boiling, you add whatever you've ordered to the hot pot. There will normally be a wide range of vegetable items, meats and seafood, all thinly sliced and prepared ready for quick boiling in the soup. If you've got your hot pot simmering away, nothing takes longer than a couple of minutes to cook. You also have a range of different sauces and flavourings on the table to spice things up, sesame paste, chili oil, chopped spring onions, soy sauce, vinegar, and many other things to mix and match to your personal taste. Hot pot is extremely popular, and I have been to this style of restaurant many, many times, but I have to confess it's not one of my favourites. I find the whole thing quite a hot and steamy experience, like trying to eat a meal while sitting in a sauna. You are basically all sitting around a great big boiling saucepan full of water, so it's going to be hot and sweaty. I guess this is why it's so popular in the North, as a way to get out of the freezing cold winters and sit somewhere warm. The method of under table heating for the hot pot pan varies from restaurant to restaurant. Some places have gas heating piped around the whole restaurant, but this can be pretty dangerous and there have been a few cases of gas explosions in these types of restaurant. The most modern restaurants have table top induction heaters, like on your cooking stove at home. But more traditional restaurants use a much more traditional method of getting heat into the middle of the table. Some old style establishments will bring out big steel pots full of smouldering coals and place this in the hole at the centre of the table. This is a practice shared with another popular type of restaurant, Korean BBQ's.

Korean BBQ is fantastic and one of my favourite, especially good if you like barbequed beef. The arrangement is similar to a hot pot restaurant, with everyone sitting around a table with a hole in the middle, but with the BBQ you need more direct heat because you're cooking the meat directly, not boiling it in a soup like in a hot pot. And whilst I love Korean BBQ, it is quite a dangerous place when the waiter just strolls in with this industrially hot crucible dangling off the end of some big tongs and he inserts it in a hole in the middle or under the table. He just strolls past everyone, with no protection, the pot comes within inches of you sometimes and you can feel the radiation off it melting the hairs on your legs. So unsafe, it would never be allowed in other countries, what if this guy tripped? Several members of your dinner party would end up in hospital with serious burns. A cooking grill goes over the top of the coals and away you go, cooking whatever you have ordered yourself fresh at the table. Tastes great, but comes at the risk of serious injury.

When we first arrived, Western fast food chains had yet

to really make their mark on Dalian. They were certainly already prominent in the big cities, but Dalian was yet to be swamped by this particular global pandemic. The one exception, and the one American fast food chain that was literally everyone in China when we arrived was Kentucky Fried Chicken. Since arriving in 1987 as the first Western fast food chain, the Chinese have really taken KFC to their hearts and their stomachs, and the franchise has grown to over 5000 restaurants across the country. They still dominate the Chinese fast food market, to the extent that many Chinese people think that KFC is actually Chinese. As the first to market, KFC learnt that success in China requires tailoring your menu to local tastes, so you will see stuff on the menu that you will never see in a KFC in the US. Their 'Dragon Twister' is a KFC take on Beijing Duck and is a must try. There were also a couple of Starbucks when we arrived, but only in the city centre. Fast food in China at the time was mainly a variety of Asian chains serving rice or noodle dishes or dumplings, including Mr Lee, Kung Fu, Dico's, Yoshinoya, and many others.

Beyond the high street version of fast food, in China, fast food also extends well into the back streets, where there are endless street corner traders stir frying and barbequing things on demand. Some people swear by street food (especially those who can't afford to dine in a proper restaurant, go figure!), but I am definitely not one of those. It's not so bad in some countries, like Singapore, where it is all regulated, and safe to eat off the street, but in China, there is no regulation, no hygiene standards and anything goes. I have had several colleagues and friends struck down by eating from these back street barbeque merchants. One of my managers, an Irish guy married to a Chinese girl (so he should have known better), was off ill for a week with terrible food poisoning. Another colleague picked up a serious liver infection from street food and was hospitalised for 6 months.

Even in the regulated side of the market, there are regular food safety scares that hit the national and international press. Remember the baby milk powder scandal that hit the headlines a few years back? Some companies were cutting milk powder with melamine (i.e. powdered plastic) to save money. Who does that? There are really some absolute scumbag sociopaths around who have zero empathy with their fellow man and all they see is a way to get a fast buck, they really don't care about the dangerous consequences of what they do. And these were state-owned companies, not back street family owned things, these were big corporations. Thousands ended up in hospital, babies died. Foreign imported baby formula became like gold dust. Prior to that there was an earlier incident with baby milk being watered down, leading to several infants dying of malnutrition.

And once I arrived in China, I found that the baby milk powder scandal was just the tip of the iceberg. During the Avian flu epidemic there was a huge scare over the safety of chicken, which affected even the Chinese institution that is KFC. There was another scandal involving the selling of expired meat, branded unfit for human consumption, to several global brands on a massive scale. In one infamous scandal, over 15,000 dead pigs were found drifting down the Huangpu River towards Shanghai. This was due to a crack-down on local pork dealers, who would buy up dead meat unfit for sale, process it illegally, and then sell it on. These dirtbags had dumped their rotting pig stocks into the river to evade the police.

But the one that did it for me was the gutter oil scandal, where unscrupulous assholes would scoop up the used, discarded cooking oil from the gutters and drains outside of restaurants, bottle it, and resell it to restaurants. That is exactly the reason why I do not eat from street vendors in China, because chances are, they are using gutter oil. Your lovely freshly stir-fried spicy Dan Dan noodles have just been cooked in oil scooped out of the gutter. Those are not freshly ground bits of pepper corn in your sauce, at best they are going to be something unrecognisable stuck on the bottom of someone's shoe, at worst it may be month old dog turd, crushed up into a fine browny-grey grit. Yum yum! Take your chances if you wish, but don't say I didn't warn you.

As I said, there were very few Western style fast food outlets in Dalian when we arrived. But over the years, one by one, they all started arriving, as these chains branched out beyond the big cities, and by the time we left there were numerous McDonalds, plus Pizza Hut, Papa Johns, Dominos, Burger King, Dunkin Donuts, and Subway all made an appearance. There was also a big expansion of Starbucks across the city over this time, to be joined by other Western and Chinese coffee houses, including Costa Coffee, Pacific Coffee, Maan Coffee, Laan Coffee, Caffe Bene, Hollys Coffee and many others, as coffee culture grew tremendously over this period, transforming China from a nation of tea drinkers into coffee drinkers in just 5 years, fuelled by the millennials. All of this change was great for us foreigners, giving us more choice and the best of both worlds, and the younger Chinese seemed to like it, but you have to question what it is doing to Chinese culture and eating habits.

As a lǎowài, Starbucks is like a little oasis of Western culture. After all the noodle shops and hot pot restaurants, just taking time out for a Starbucks latte is a real relaxer for me. Even though the place is still full of Chinese people of course, it's just the familiar ambience and décor that makes the whole experience a respite from the cultural onslaught going on when you step back out onto the street.

Julie and I are not big eaters of fast food, and back in the Western world, we would rarely enter a McDonalds, but to be fair, in Dalian, McDonalds did change our life. Not something we would normally eat when sober, but the 5am McDonalds breakfast became an integral part of our Friday or Saturday evening all-nighters. After stumbling out of the late night drinking dens at 5 or 6 in the morning, piling into a taxi to head to the 24 hour Mickey D's just seemed a natural extension of the night and became an absolute necessity to satisfy our munchies. And pulling an 'all-nighter' became completely 'de rigueur' amongst our circle of friends. What always surprised me was that there were still actually people around at 5am in McDonald's. These were generally a few locals who had just got up, so I'm sure it was a real surprise for them to see a bunch of drunken foreigners stumbling around their local breakfast place. And by the time we made it back to the apartment, the sun had always come up (hence 'all-nighter').

CHAPTER 7

SNOWFLAKE BEER FOR GIRLS (OR THE DRINKING CULTURE IN CHINA)

All this writing about food is making me thirsty. You certainly can't sit down in China for dinner with friends or colleagues without having something alcoholic thrust at you, usually several different kinds of things.

In China, the most (in)famous drink of them all is Bái Jiǔ, which literally means white alcohol. And the most well-known brand of bái jiǔ is called Maotai, so named from the town in which it was first made. Bái jiǔ is a super strong spirit (40-65% alcohol) distilled from fermented sorghum (no, I didn't know what sorghum was either). Sorghum is a type of flowering grass, native to Africa, Asia and Australasia (which is presumably why we haven't heard of it in the West), used for animal feed and as a source of biofuel. Bái Jiǔ is a complex drink, and just like whisky and other spirits, there are many different types. Some taste like supping on the industrial waste stream from a paint thinners factory. Others taste like storm run-off from a field of rotten cabbages, complete with copious amounts of pesticides sprayed on them to add an extra chemical zest. Yet others taste like used drain cleaner. But they all have one thing in common, they are all a serious challenge to your taste buds and to your liver.

Maotai, or some other expensive brand of bái jiǔ is a must have at any Chinese banquet. The host will bring it into the room like a much revered ancient relic and place it centre stage on the lazy Susan. Fortunately the traditional glass that goes with Maotai is no bigger than a thimble, which helps, because you will be expected to gānbēi whenever someone toasts you, and there is a lot of toasting going on at a Chinese dinner, so those little thimbles-full soon add up. Gānbēi literally means 'dry glass', so you are expected to drain it empty in one go whenever challenged. You will normally be given a small jug that is filled up frequently, to allow you and others to keep topping up your thimble glass. You cannot escape, your hosts will be swarming around you like beggars around a tourist. It always amazes me how quickly the drinking starts, after only a couple of dishes have been placed in the table, people are starting to get up and walk around and start toasting each other. And once this happens it is not long before most people are up on their feet following course, and the dinner is only half way through by that point. After a few thimbles-full, inevitably the bigger glasses come out and the drinking starts to get serious.

I recall one Chinese New Year company party I attended where we were gānbēi-ing bái jiǔ out of highball glasses, that's 20 times the volume of the little thimble glasses. I stupidly made up this drinking game to see who could pick up the glass with their mouth, without using their hands, and gānbēi the whole thing, which I discovered I was pretty good at. This really started a trend that night and everyone was challenging me to it. Plenty of bái jiǔ on the floor by the end of the evening, plus a few broken glasses. No idea how much we drank but it was a difficult night. I think everyone survived, though my memory is a little hazy about that night.

The thing with alcohol is that it is an acquired taste. You remember as a teenager your first beer or your first whisky? Not such a good experience. But with persistence, eventually you end up loving it. Bái jiǔ is different. I have drunk a lot of bái jiǔ over the years, some nights, copious quantities, especially at all those Chinese New Year company parties. But no matter how much I drink, I have never developed a taste for it. It is still as disgusting to me today as it was the first time I experienced it. The local Chinese love it of course, I guess they just started much earlier than me with it. One of the worst things with bái jiǔ is that the bad experience seriously lingers. If you have been lucky enough to endure a full on bái jiǔ night, then you will know what I mean. Your mouth will likely feel like someone else has vomited in it. But this is only the beginning of your experience. The next day, after a heavy night's chemically induced sleep, you will be awakened to the aroma of stale bái jiǔ. You will find that the taste and the smell of the stuff has spread throughout your entire body and seeped out of every pore. You just taste and smell it all day long. A really gross lingering experience, so be warned.

Another baijiu lingering effect of all my years in China that still persists to this day, is that I now have to be very careful whenever I'm ordering drinks on vacation at a beach resort anywhere in the world. My go to island drink is the Mai Tai, a beautiful rum based cocktail. I got a taste for this in Hawaii, where Julie & I got married, and have since vacationed there many times. But since my China days, whenever I'm ordering it, I still find myself saying Maotai instead of Mai Tai. I quickly put the order right though.

But China is not all about bái jiǔ, a more palatable alternative at half the strength (<20% alcohol) is huáng jiǔ, meaning yellow alcohol, normally brewed from rice. This is much easier on the stomach and doesn't burn as it goes down, like bái jiǔ. So if your Chinese hosts bring out the huáng jiǔ instead, then be sure to thank them profusely.

Unlike the spirits, Chinese beer can be pretty good. The world famous Tsingtao brand is everywhere you turn in China, Every bar, every restaurant and every hotel stocks Tsingtao. Tsingtao is named after the city it was originally made in, which is Qingdao. Yes I know it's not spelt quite the same, but that's just a translation thing, the Chinese characters for the city and the beer are exactly the same. The brand is over a hundred years old. The brewery was founded in 1903 by an Anglo-German team. Maybe Chinese-English translation was done differently then, or maybe they just couldn't spell. Anyway, everyone says Qingdao, even though it's written Tsingtao. Qingdao is a beautiful coastal city in Shandong province, less than one hour flight from Dalian. We were lucky enough to have the chance to visit the city, a really fabulous place, lots of decent beaches, interesting places to visit and beautiful landscapes. But no visit to the city is complete without visiting the original Tsingtao brewery and museum. This is probably the best brewery tour I have done in the world. Very interesting. You get to tour the old factory and museum and the new factory and have beer tasting of course. Tsingtao actually brews many types of beer. The locals claim it's the local water that gives the beer its great taste, and subsequently Tsingtao made anywhere else is just not the same. I drank plenty whilst I was there, maybe they have a point. One of their staple brands is pretty weak, at 2.5% alcohol, and hardly worth the effort. But the rest of their brands are great, especially the 4.5%+ beers. I was told by friends before I visited the brewery that you can actually buy beer in a plastic bag to take home, though I didn't see any of this going on. A pretty neat idea, and way ahead of its time at saving on packaging. Maybe they've discontinued it or maybe it's just for the locals.

There are other brands of beer of course in China. The other big brands are Harbin and Snow beer. In Beijing, Yanjing is popular. Question; what's the best selling beer in the world? You will be amazed, it's Snow beer. What, you've never heard of it? I'm not kidding, just look it up. It's only sold inside China but it's the best selling beer in the world. Just shows how many people drink beer in China. Whenever I see Snow beer it makes me laugh, because the actual translation on the label is 'snowflake' beer. Doesn't sound a very manly name for a beer does it, sounds like a range of beers brewed especially for little girls. The word for beer in Chines is píjiŭ. After Nĭhăo it's the second most well-known Chinese word by foreigners, but I guess that's no surprise. Píjiŭ is said to be a loanword, that is, it is supposed to sound phonetically like saying the word beer. On first hearing, it probably doesn't sound much like it, but once you get to know the sounds of the Chinese language, you can start to hear the origins of where the tones for the word come from.

If you do business in China, you definitely need a strong stomach and an even stronger liver. The drinking culture is prodigious. The company Chinese New Year party is particularly challenging. You have to go round and toast every table in the room. I attended many such events over the years. The most memorable and challenging of them was a New Year Party for one of our Shanghai companies. There were 600 people in the room, 10 to a table. So we were faced with toasting 60 tables individually. A serious drinking challenge in itself, but compounded by the fact that this was a lunch time party, and we had another party to go to that evening! I certainly earned my salary that day. I used to dread Chinese New Year season. As directors of the company, we would be expected to visit all our Chinese companies and attend their annual parties. We had about a dozen companies around the country, so it took some serious logistics and some serious drinking to get through them all. About 10 days of continuous partying. Often with 2 parties on the same day. It took several weeks of recovery time.

There is plenty of etiquette surrounding drinking at formal occasions in China. It's normal to wait for the most important member of the dinner party, either the host or the guest of honour, to start drinking first. You will be able to spot the most important person in the room because they are usually the one sitting directly opposite the door. One such form of drinking etiquette is when you toast someone. You are supposed to show deference to a more senior person by holding your glass lower than the other person when you clink your glasses together for a toast. Seems good logic in this to me and I always try to do this. But the situation inevitably arises when they hold their glass lower than yours but you want to show respect to them and move your glass below theirs and then they respond by lowering their glass even further. If this carries on, you can find yourself both on your knees before one of you gives up and accepts the respect from the other.

It was evident during my time in China that there was a growing wine culture there, fuelled by the rise of the middle class, with more disposal income, looking for the finer things of life to spend it on. Even before I arrived there, I had heard of big Chinese wine brands like Great Wall. I discovered that Great Wall, along with Changyu, were two of the biggest producers, with the widest offerings, from low cost value brands right up to expensive gold medal winning labels, and the shelves of the local supermarket was always full of them. The cheap to mid-priced bottles I would buy occasionally in my early days there were absolute piss. Even bottles around 200RMB, which is 4 times what I would pay in the UK for a bottle of supermarket wine, were so bad that I had to pour them down the sink straight after uncorking. Just the smell was enough to make you feel sick, and the taste was absolutely indescribable. I don't know what it was, but it wasn't wine.

To get a decent bottle of wine in China in the early days you needed to pay a lot of money or buy foreign. Given the geography, the Australian wine producers had been targeting the Chinese market for years and fortunately were readily available, but again, they were market priced for the nouveau riche Chinese, with inflated prices to add a sense of quality and luxury to elevate the status of wine as a product. Cheap supermarket Australian brands back home were marketed as high quality expensive brands in China. This is what you can do when you have a brand new market to attack.

Foreign Wine producers must be rubbing their hands with glee over the Chinese market. They have the biggest population on the planet, with money to spend, but at the same time, most of the potential customers are completely ignorant about wine, and all ripe for educating by whomever gets in first. This has attracted many foreign and indigenous investors and I was always bumping into visitors and expats from the wine trade over there. Julie and

I went to some very memorable wine tasting events put on by French vineyards trying to get a foothold in the Chinese market, get there name known and bag some lucrative contracts supplying the big hotels. These were incredibly grand affairs, with lavish tasting menus to accompany all the wines on offer.

There has been a rapid increase in new vineyards opening up in China in the last few years, especially in the West of the country in Shanxi province, where the best growing conditions can be found for wine grapes. Most of the existing wine production capacity in China is along the east coast, in Shandong and Hebei Provinces, with some down in the South West in Yunnan, with each regional climate favouring different grape varieties. Many of the newly established vineyards entice foreign wine growing experts over to help them set up and try to bring their product up to national and eventually international standards. There is plenty of money to be made by wine growing experts in China. The millions of investment dollars have also targeted the establishment of a wine tourism industry, with many of the new vineyards having wonderful French style chateaus as their centrepiece to host wine tours and tastings.

There were two expats in Dalian that had set up wine import businesses, bringing in product from their home countries, one French guy and the other an Argentinian. Both were very active on the expat social scene. The French guy was one of the biggest piss heads I have ever met. He was good at his subject and hosted some fine tasting soirees, but he was one of those classic guys that likes his own product too much. Whenever you saw him around town in the evening he was completely drunk. The first 5 or 6 times I met him socially, on separate occasions, after each time he never remembered me because he was so drunk and just couldn't remember anything.

The growth in the wine trade was clearly visible on the streets, with more and more wine shops opening up each year. By the time we left Dalian, almost every street in the city centre had its own wine shop. But even now, it can still be a frustrating experience ordering wine, even in some 5 star hotels. The waitresses are usually poorly trained and don't know how to pour or serve, and often more than half the wines listed on their drinks menu are not available. It's even worse in restaurants, where many still keep their red wine in the fridge and serve their white wine at room temperature. So despite the investment and obvious growth in the industry, the Chinese still have a lot to learn about wine. For many, they still think there are only two types of wine, red and white. But things are improving, and today, the average Chinese produced wine is certainly getting better in the supermarkets, though no less expensive, and the range of foreign imports has grown in availability, which is good for the consumer. But a primary factor in the frequently disappointing wine experience in hotels and restaurant is still the endemic trade in 'fake' wines, such that whatever the label says on the bottle, you can never really be sure what you are drinking.

If all this alcohol is too much to take, or if you're a teetotaller, then don't despair, China doesn't have to all be about drinking alcohol. You can always wash the taste away with some vinegar if you like. In Chinese, the word for vinegar is cù. But it is not the kind of vinegar we know in the West. Cù applies to a whole range of vinegar types, some you mix 50:50 with soy sauce to make a delicious dipping sauce for dumplings, but others refer to a tasty drinking variety, such as apple vinegar, which tastes a little like non-alcoholic cider, so pretty nice. We actually have something similar in the West called apple cider vinegar, used in salad dressings. Cù also means jealousy in Chinese, particularly relating to love rivalries. The phrase 'to drink vinegar' is used if a girl is jealous of her boyfriend flirting with another girl. So be warned if you say you want to try drinking some vinegar.

If you think drinking vinegar is strange, then you'll be seriously challenged by some of the stuff that you're served up once you get out into the real China, once you get away from Shanghai, Beijing and other large civilised cities. One of my colleagues ended up in hospital with kidney problems from drinking a glass of fresh deer blood mixed with wine that he was offered at one business dinner out in the sticks. Seriously, why would anyone drink that, it seems so dangerous. But some Chinese swear by it. They believe that drinking raw deer blood nourishes your own blood and improves your health. Some claim it also increases your virility, and the drink was certainly served along with the phrase 'good for man', and with the cheeky nudge and wink that always accompanies all things that are meant to improve male virility. And in your time in China and across the whole of Asia, you will be presented with many weird and wonderful things, usually of the food variety rather than drinks, which are meant to be 'good for man' (nudge, nudge, wink, wink). Once these appear on the table, they are almost inevitably penis shaped, or often actual penises of various animals. I have been presented with plenty of bull and donkey penises in my time, but that's another story.

But the ultimate in odd, everyday drinks that you will discover in China is not alcoholic at all, it is plain old water. One of your first everyday experiences when moving to China is that when you want a glass of water, it will be served to you hot. The Chinese believe that drinking hot water, instead of cold or room temperature, is better for digestion and easier on the stomach. In all my years growing up in the West no one ever heated up plain water to drink it. We only ever boiled water to make tea and coffee. But this simple act of serving plain water hot throws you off balance. It is another example of how China challenges everything you thought you knew about how to live your everyday life, about how you think everyday things should be done. It is such an incredibly simple thing, serving water hot instead of room temperature, but immediately the logic of it makes sense. It may seem odd to you as a Westerner, but immediately you get it, immediately you realise there are other ways to approach even the simplest of things. An attitude that has far reaching consequences on how you approach everything and another valuable life lesson from China.

DR ANDY WYNN

CHAPTER 8

DUCK IN A PLASTIC BAG (OR THE JOYS OF TRAVELLING IN CHINA)

One morning, the driver and I were on our way to work as usual. Mr Fang and I stopped in a line of traffic just outside the city, heading towards the new factory I had built. We were both lazily looking out at the car in front, me half asleep in the passenger seat. Mr Fang nudged me and pointed. I looked ahead at the car in front. We both looked back at each other with our mouths open. We both did a double take, and straight out came our iPhones to capture the spectacle ahead of us.

The car in front had a large duck taped securely onto the lid of the trunk. He was happily sat there in the middle of the back of the car, looking around. Almost the whole of his body had been stuck down to the car body with masses of industrial grade parcel tape. Someone had made sure this duck wasn't going to fall off during the car journey. The duck seemed amazingly calm about its situation. I can only imagine what was in the driver's head when he taped his duck to his car. Was it a compassion thing? Did he want to give his bird some air and keep him cool during the drive? Otherwise, why didn't he just put him in a box inside the car? The driver had seemingly thought about the duck's well-being because he had given the duck two companions. Either side of the duck taped to the middle of the trunk lid, were two plastic grocery bags hanging down, seemingly fixed to some point inside the trunk, and in each bag was placed another duck. Their bodies were hidden within the plastic bags and just their heads and necks were poking out. These two birds also seemed pretty happy with their lot and were looking around keenly as if they were on a school trip.

So there we were, sat in traffic, staring at this sedan with the three ducks hanging off the back. A very surreal moment. What can you say? The car was just a standard sedan, not a goods vehicle. I can only speculate as to where the driver was going, why he chose to tape his ducks to the back of his car, and what he was going to do with them once he reached his destination. Was he driving them out to the countryside and going to release his ducks into the wild to lead a happy natural life? Or was he on his way to sell them to a restaurant to end up in a cooking pot that evening. Maybe the taping down of the bird onto the car body was an efficient way of plucking it. I cannot imagine, given how efficiently the duck was taped down, that once they ripped off all the tape it would have many feathers left on its body. Though I guess the most likely reason for the ducks being taped to the car was probably that the trunk was already full.

Imagine the situation. We were sat in traffic that was backed up to get onto the local highway, where the cars would be travelling upwards of 100 km/h. That must surely be quite an exhilarating ride for the three ducks, talk about wind through your hair, or rather feathers in their case. We never got to find out the story behind the ducks of course. The traffic moved on, the car and the ducks headed of and that was the last we saw of them. I've told this story a few times to friends and had people in fits of giggles after showing them the amazing pictures from that day. It usually ends up with someone saying, 'what did they use to tape the duck down? Duck(t) tape?'

This whole episode epitomises the travel experience in Asia for me. There's always a real sense of things being out of place, usually with a large dose of discomfort, you are often left wondering whether you will ever actually arrive at your destination, and sometimes you find yourself questioning why you even started the journey in the first place. Many is the time travelling around China that I have felt a lot like that duck taped to the back of the car.

China is a big, big country, as big as the whole of the USA. Yet China has only one time zone, whilst the continental USA has four. The time zone thing certainly helps when you are travelling around China, making things simpler, one less thing to worry about when changing flights, but I'm sure it's a bit of a bugger for those living in the far West in the Winter, when the sun doesn't come up until 10am at some times of the year.

But the Chinese government have been tackling the challenge of immense size at a pace, laying out massive infrastructure projects across the country, improving links from the developed and highly populated East to the more rural West of the country all the time. Better to get the raw material wealth out from the West to where it's needed. And it's not just the West it is opening up, they have been looking even beyond that and opening up better trade routes through their neighbours to the East, with their 'Belt and Road' initiative, laying new mega-long rail routes out through Kazakhstan, through Russia and out towards Europe, building a modern version of the ancient Silk Road. They continue to extend their road network, laying kilometres of highways at a pace never seen before on the planet. China has nearly 140,000 km of expressway road network now, the world's largest expressway system by length, having overtaken the US Interstate Highway System in 2011.

China leads the way in modern and high speed rail. China also now has the world's longest high speed rail network, which at 25,000 km, accounts for two thirds of the entire world's high speed rail tracks. This is on top of their standard speed rail system, which has already reached over 100,000 km of track. Around 4,000 km of new track is laid every year, with nearly 90% of this being high-speed. High speed rail means the carriage will be travelling at between 250–350 km/h, which is similar to the take-off speed of a passenger jet, so it's pretty fast. And it's this that has made high speed rail instrumental in opening up Chinese cities and providing a realistic rival to air travel between cities in China. In fact, I find the whole experience of travelling on high speed rail very much like travelling by aircraft. I have taken many high speed rail journeys now within China. When you get to the high speed rail station, you get a real feeling of being at an airport. They are on a similar scale, there are similar facilities, they are laid out in a similar manner and waiting at the departure gate to walk onto the platform is pretty much the same experience as you go through at an airport. But the actual journey can be much more comfortable, with bigger seats and more spacious carriages compared to in the cabin of an aircraft. You can actually get up and stretch your legs, you can get some work done and you can even pre-order meals to be delivered straight to your seat. I say 'can be', because it really depends on the timing of your train. Early morning commuter trains can be ultra-packed, and there are increasing incidents of passengers getting into fisticuffs over seats, even though they are pre-assigned.

The Chinese government's mega-infrastructure projects are not just confined to China itself. They have been exporting their highway and high speed rail expertise all over the world, investing heavily in infrastructure projects across Africa and South America.

The other thing you notice when travelling around the country for business or pleasure, is just how many new airports are being built. It is amazing how often you land in a new city you've never heard of for a business trip, only to discover you are arriving at a huge, brand new, shiny airport, bigger than you have back home in the West. China already has over 200 commercial airports, and have already started work on another 66, due to open in the next 5 years, with many more planned beyond that.

But the challenges for China of moving so many people around are apparent every time you travel, especially around Spring Festival time, when an estimated 3 billion trips are made by road, rail and airplane over the festive period. We learnt very quickly to avoid travelling at such busy times, when the infrastructure becomes log jammed and facilities strain under the sheer numbers trying to pass through them. I experienced this first hand on one trip to Xian, the home of the famous Terracotta Warriors. We spent a few days visiting the city for a long weekend, to see all the famous sights. I was really impressed with the city, it has so much more to offer than just the Warriors. The medieval city walls are amazing, and perfect for a bicycle ride around the whole city to get your bearings. And there are plenty of amazing places to visit in the city centre, the Big Wild Goose Pagoda, Shaanxi History Museum, Drum and Bell Towers, the Muslim quarter, and many others. Definitely one of my favourite cities in China. The timing of our trip meant that our final day coincided with Labour Day, a national public holiday on 1st May shared with many other countries around the world. This was to be the first time we had ventured out as tourists beyond our home city of Dalian on a public holiday, in mainland China, and definitely the last. We decided to have an easy last day, and walk the 2 km into the city centre from our hotel to see the Drum and Bell towers. By the time we got there, it was already pretty busy on the streets, which I expected because of the Labour Day holiday, but over the next couple of hours, more and more people arrived, building up the numbers to the point that where we were in the centre, I had never seen such a densely packed crowd of people in my life. Much worse than any mega-outdoor concert festival. It was literally shoulder to shoulder. It was really impossible for us to continue our sightseeing as it was such tiring work trying to shove past all the crowds, so we decided to make our way back to the hotel. But even walking back was a real challenge. At one point the pedestrians were so densely packed on the pavement, and so tightly compressed shoulder to shoulder, that I was literally squeezed upwards by the crowd and carried along with my feet dangling below me. I have never experienced such a sense of being out of control in such a densely packed crowd of people before, and it is a scary feeling. Fortunately the crowd was meandering in the direction of our hotel, so we got shunted along the human river and spat out at the end of the street as the crowd thinned a little. It was quite an experience and brought home to me the challenges the civil authorities have of trying to manage such a densely populated and huge population.

Chinese airports are notorious the world over for flight delays. If you spend any time in Chinese airports, then you will get used very quickly to hearing one particular phrase over the loudspeakers again and again, 'Wŏmen Bàoqiàn….', which means 'we apologise for….'. I soon learnt that if your plane departs within one hour of the scheduled time, then that is on time for China and you should be thankful. Delays are usually down to one of three things, weather, technical problems and the Chinese military. The most common but weirdest 'Wŏmen Bàoqiàn' announcement is when they apologise for the delay in the scheduled departure time of your flight, 'due to the late arrival of the incoming plane'. Huh? Yes, but why was the incoming plane delayed? That's what everyone wants to know. This type of announcement is just a classic case of non-information and only fuels passenger frustration.

China has some big weather, it's a vast country, it has vast open spaces for winds to gather speed, it has vast mountain ranges to create big thermals and a huge North-South span encompassing vast differences in ambient temperature. It suffers typhoons up and down its East coast every year and devastating monsoon rains along its south coast. It is not surprising that weather causes the occasional flight delay.

Up in the north east, as a coastal city, the number one problem for Dalian airport is fog. The first year we moved there, the fog was so bad in the spring that the airport was closed for 5 days solidly. No planes in, no planes out. Imagine the disruption to people's lives and to business. This was in the days before the high speed rail track to Shenyang had opened, so there were pretty much zero options for you if you had an urgent trip to make outside the province. In those days, a train journey to Beijing would take around 20 hours. There is no direct route possible because of the geography, Dalian is on the tip of a massive promontory sticking out into the sea. Land transport is only possible northwards, and Beijing is due west. I was extremely lucky that I had no business trips planned during those 5 days, so I could just sit it out at home. But an American friend of mine traveling back home to Dalian was not so lucky. He arrived in Beijing from his international flight on the first day of the fog in Dalian. After sitting at the airport for several hours, his domestic flight was finally cancelled, and they shipped everyone off to some crappy hotel in the middle of nowhere, miles from the airport. It was late, so the restaurant was closed and there were no shops nearby, so he told me it was a pretty hungry night for him. Anyhow, the next day the passengers were all bussed back to the airport for their rescheduled flight, and sat around all day again waiting for news of their flight to Dalian. Once again, because of the ongoing fog, the flight was cancelled after several hours of waiting and everyone was again bussed off to the same crappy hotel. This went on for the full 5 days. I can't imagine how he felt.

Whilst I have never experienced quite this degree of delay, I have had similar but milder experiences, only one or two overnight stays. But after the first couple of years, I got wise to how these things always played out. The way the lack of information on your scheduled flight was a way to keep the crowd of passengers quiet, subdued and expectant. The hotel they took you to was always really poor, no matter which class of seat you had purchased. And if you're travelling alone, they always try to pair you up with some complete stranger to squeeze you in two to a room. After about 2 hours delay they are legally required to feed the passengers, so out comes a huge industrial box of airplane meals for everyone. They always seem to time it perfectly for when you have just become fed up enough of sitting around waiting and you start to take a stroll around the airport to stretch your legs, so very often I miss this particular box of delights. How these flight companies treat their passengers really sucks. Sure, we all understand that things go wrong out of their control, and we all would rather delay our trip if it means a safe trip, but delays happen so often, you would think that these airlines would have their fall back procedures down to a tee. But in reality it always seems like the team on the ground struggle and are making things up as they go along.

One major issue with Chinese airlines is that all the staff and crew are just so young. The flight crew always seem like they are in their early 20s. I am sure they are reasonably trained, but when it comes to dealing with things outside the ordinary, they lack the experience and maturity to deal with it. When passengers are ranting and raving at them, and I've seen that happen many times, they just clam up and cower, usually while the rest of the passengers are videoing it all on their mobile phones. But a young cabin crew is a natural consequence of the massive economic boom that China has experienced over the last 20-30 years. Many of the older generation in China has grown up without ever setting foot on an aircraft. Their generation has no experience of such things, no understanding of even the basics of using airports. It's the same with driving. It's the reason that driving on Chinese roads is so dangerous. There are a lot of cars on the roads of China now, especially with China being the number one car manufacturer in the world. But the previous generation has no experience of car ownership and zero driving skills. The average car owner today in China is often the first generation of their family to own and drive a car. There is no legacy of car ownership and zero driving skills to be passed on by parents. It is hard for a Westerner to comprehend this situation, hard to appreciate the dramatic change in lifestyle that has been dropped onto the Chinese way of life in such a short time. Consequently, the previous generation are probably untrainable in modern jobs like aircraft cabin crew, and hence the propensity for young staff in all these types of job, who have grown up with modern engineering and technology around them and so have a deeper intrinsic understanding of such things.

So as I said, I got wise to the delay procedures, to the sequence of events and decisions that are enacted every time. And after the first couple of years suffering these things, any time there was a delay I would make a judgement on the things they said and the way they said them and make a 'should I stay or should I go' decision, because I knew what was coming. I would rather extract myself from the mayhem at the airport and retire to some comfortable 4 star hotel, relax a bit, and get some work done, than be dumped into the usual shitty zero star hotel and smelly stranger room share that was inevitably looming. A day lost is usually not the end of the world in business, you can always have the meeting on the phone the next day. I have discovered over the years that keeping your stress levels low is really important for your health and sanity and actually helps you do a better job.

As I mentioned in Chapter 1, we experienced our very first flight delay in China on the very first domestic flight I had booked for Julie's first trip to China, to travel to Dalian for a pre-visit to see if she would be okay moving there. We arrived into Beijing from our international flight, only to endure what I have described above. Several hours sat at the airport, a cancelled flight to Dalian, and being shipped off to a crappy hotel in the middle of the night. Not a great start to our 6 years in China. I was trying to show Julie the best of everything, with business class travel and five star hotels, to show China in the best light. The night at the crappy hotel was not a great start, but fortunately it did not affect her decision to move with me to China, so all was well in the end, but it was a taste of things to come.

On another occasion, Julie and I were flying from Shanghai to Dalian, but due to heavy fog in Dalian, our plane was diverted to Shenyang, which is 400 km north of Dalian. They made us all wait at Shenyang airport, listening for news of our flight, but as I said, I was wise by then. And also, the high speed train route between Shenyang and Dalian had been opened a few months previously. So we took the decision to bail out. We collected our baggage, got a taxi to the high speed train station and was pulling in to Dalian station 2 hours later. I kept checking the flight information on my phone regularly to see if I had made the right decision, and sure enough, just as we arrived in Dalian, there it was; 'flight cancelled'. What a smart move. I was feeling pretty smug with myself, but that's the value of experience.

One of the reasons that I don't mind making the decision to bail out of our flight these days at the first signs of any serious delay or cancellation is that the domestic flights are just so cheap. It's not like you're losing a lot of money. And this leads us to the second of the main reasons for flight delays; technical difficulties. We all know that the airline business is massively competitive, and particularly for short haul journeys, where there always seems to be a price war going on for bums on seats in Asia and Europe (though not in the US yet). This has driven prices down to some ludicrous levels for non-peak travel times, to such an extent in Europe that it is sometimes more expensive to travel to and from the airport than it is to take the flight.

It's normal to fly from Dalian to Shanghai for less than $100 one way, and often less than $50 or lower if you pick one of the really no frills airlines. There are some European flights I have paid for that cost me less than $20. In the case of the European approach, the ticket face price is very misleading, as by the time you have paid extra for hold luggage and extra for a drink and snack on the flight, it can easily add up to $100 anyway, but there is always this nagging feeling about what else is the airline trying to save money on that you cannot see? What is your $20 'not' paying for? i.e. what about the maintenance of the plane? Safety is everything when you are going to sit in a machine that's going to be cruising at 30,000 feet above the ground. And there are some things that you just don't really want cheap versions of. Would you want cheap brain surgery? Or cheap heart surgery? So whenever the 'Wǒmen Bàoqiàn' announcement is due to 'technical difficulties', it always makes me question are we paying enough for our flights?

Generally the Chinese budget airlines haven't got to the stage yet of charging you for every little thing separately, which makes for less complicated journey. Though the choice of food on the flights is getting ever narrower and smaller. But I will say this for some of the Chines airlines, when they bring you hot food, it is hot, not like in the West, where by the time you receive it, it is normally lukewarm. In China, I actually look forward to their Chicken and Rice appearing, it's pretty good.

With such a massive commercial airline market in China, and expanding at a rapid rate, there are just so many airlines in China to choose from, including some with weird and wonderful names. Do you really want to fly something called 'Lucky Air'? I for one don't really want luck involved if I'm flying. And as for 'Okay Airways'? 'How was your flight? It was okay'. Although I think we'd all be better on 'Joy Air'. Most of them are named after the city or region that they are based at, but inevitably there are so many companies trying their hand in this market, that some of them don't last long in business. Almost every time you go to book a flight, you will see one of the options being an airline you have never heard of before, such is the number of airlines flying in China and around Asia these days. In 2018, Chinese airlines carried over 600 million passengers on domestic and international routes, 50% more than only 5 years ago. This figure is due to grow further within the next 5 years to surpass even the US market and become the number one aviation market in the world. And the Chinese government is pouring money into the industry to fuel this growth, investing in developing its own aircraft building industry and supporting infrastructure, as they currently still have to buy all their aircraft from the big European and US manufacturers. China did this year, launch their very first fully domestically manufactured passenger jet, so it is only a matter of time before this capability builds into a self-sustaining industry.

When it comes to the flight experience itself in China, there are a few budget airlines with a unique approach in the cabin, which makes for a distinctive flying experience. On one budget airline that we flew from Dalian to Xian, a three and a half hour flight, they were not content with making you pay for everything on your flight, they also spent most of the time bombarding you with adverts over the PA system, constantly trying to sell you things throughout the flight. I guess they have a real captive audience and they are trying to exploit that as much as possible. But it doesn't make for a relaxing flight, so never again.

The endeavour of taking a flight in China has a very

different flavour to that in the West. The Chinese have developed their own set of passenger etiquette and rules of engagement in the cabin. The first thing that most shocks a Westerner on a Chinese flight, is when the aircraft starts to come in to land. It is amazing how many people start to get up out of their seats and start getting their luggage out of the overhead bins as the plane is descending fast. This happens every single time on a domestic Chinese flight, with the stewardess frantically shouting at these people to sit down. Some of these people have also developed a sly trick with their hand luggage to move them closer to the exit for deboarding. As they board, they will drop their luggage into the first class overhead bins, and then head for their seat at the back of the plane. When the plane starts its landing approach, they will get out of their seats, wander down the aisle and open the overhead bin in first class. When the stewardess inevitably shouts at them to sit down, they just plonk themselves down in the nearest available seat, usually in first class. Hey presto, they are at the front of the plane ready to make a sharp exit with their hand luggage. A canny plan for them and they can feel pretty smug as they exit the airplane first, though not very socially aware. And it's not just the adults who wander around the plane as it is landing. It amazes me how often I see parents let their young children squirm around their seat without their seat belt on, and often standing up to look out of the window as the plane is landing. Not very responsible parents, and I've seen a few kids buffeted around on landing.

There does seem to be a general disregard for safety and respect for the rules and regulations of travelling in an aircraft cabin by a small but significant slice of the Chinese population. These are no doubt also the same people that have those massive arguments with airport staff when there are delays. I have seen and heard some mega bust ups in airports and on airplanes in my time in China, some that spilled out of the plane and onto the tarmac on some occasions. When there are big flight delays, tempers flare, and it is an unfortunately all too common regular news item in the Chinese media to read of airline crews and ground staff being assaulted, mobs of angry passengers storming runways, and people opening emergency exit doors when they get stuck on an aircraft. Such behaviour, although shocking and plainly wrong, and sometimes very scary, has an important message to tell about the development of the consumer society in China. People are only just waking up to the concept that as consumers they are entitled to certain rights. But China does not yet have in place the necessary institutions, like consumer rights groups, to deal with this in a structured, orderly, and legal manner. So just like in the Wild West, the Chinese public are starting to make up their own rules.

I have also seen and endured some disgusting habits on Chinese flights. People with their feet up on the seat in front, sometimes dangling over. I turned round in one seat to see someone's foot sticking out from behind, level with my face. I just battered it down with my inflight magazine. I had another guy in the seat in front of me stretching his arms up over his head and grabbing his headrest with both his hands. Not normally a problem, but this guy's hands were stretched so far round that they were covering my TV screen. I battered him down as well. I had another guy dump the remains of his inflight meal tray on top of mine when he'd finished, even though I had not.

But fortunately, the vast majority of Chinese people are just people, like the world over. Like most, they are friendly, genuine and pleasant, regardless of their level of education. I had one charming guy sitting next to me once who had clearly never been on a plane before. He was quite old and a rural farmer type guy. He was very friendly, but very excited to be on an aircraft. I had the window seat, but he was clearly very excited and kept looking out of the window, and kept craning right across me all the time, so I swapped seats with him of course. But I must say, even though I have travelled 1000s of flights in my time, I still get a kick out of looking out of the window at the amazing views you get from the air. It is something I never tire of.

And so we come to the third and the real underlying cause of the majority of delays in China. The real problem is that the Chinese military controls 80 percent of the country's airspace. So even though China is a massive country, with massive air space, the 20 percent open for commercial flights is just too small to cope with demand. So delays are inevitable, and the whole situation is only going to get worse with the continuing growth in passenger flights. You know the Chinese military are the cause of your delay when the 'Wǒmen Bàoqiàn' announcement is simply announcing a delay to your scheduled departure time with no reason. It is almost always accompanied by delays to several other flights all around the same time. Many times under these circumstances, I have sat at the gate in Dalian airport, watching the military jets take off from the runway. But no one says anything of course.

The nearest big city to Dalian is not actually in China at all. Seoul is only 50 minutes flight time east of the city. This situation leads to two very special quirks of air travel in the region, both of which are related to South Korea's massive beauty industry. The first is due to the South Korean cosmetic surgery industry and the second due to their cosmetics industry.

Seoul has become one of the leading cosmetic surgery destinations on the planet. Koreans have got their procedures down to a fine art, and with so many surgeries to choose from walking down the streets of the capital, it is now routine for people to pop in during their lunch hour for a quick eye tuck. This makes nipping over from Dalian a very popular trip with the local ladies. When flying the Dalian-Seoul route, every return flight will have one or more women with their face, eyes and/or nose wrapped in bandages sat on the plane, guaranteed. But this trip makes for a unique problem for these ladies, one that can cause a few unexpected difficulties for those who have not thought ahead. It is not uncommon for these ladies to get stopped at immigration when trying to exit the country after their surgery and get back home, because they no longer look like their passport photo. Doh!

The return trip from Seoul was also always a massive hassle for all of us, not just the ladies with the cosmetic surgery, but for a different reason. Every time you arrived at the departure gate, you would notice straight away how there were lots of people with huge amounts of hand luggage in the form of several bulging shopping bags each. Typically there would be between 30 and 40% of the passengers armed with these shopping bags and of course that made for a difficult boarding process, with everyone fighting for overhead luggage space that was never going to be enough for all the extra hand luggage people were squeezing on board. I frequently sat by young ladies that had boarded last so had no more room for their bags and had to sit on the flight with their remaining bags perched uncomfortably over them, squashing them into their seat, looking like they had an airbag that had already deployed. But it did usually spill over into your seat space. Fortunately it was not a long flight, only 50 minutes. So why all the shopping bags?

All these people were travelling to South Korea to buy

duty free Korean cosmetics and other products to sell back home in China on their TaoBao shop. Korean cosmetics are considered the best quality in the world and are in high demand right across the Asian region. Thanks to the strengthening of the Chinese currency, a trip to Korea to buy duty free cosmetics could easily double your money when sold back in China. These people would fly in and out on the same day, and not even leave the airport, just buying everything duty free. Flying back on these flights was always a real pain in the arse with all the pushing and shoving, so I was grateful a couple of years ago when the South Korean government imposed limits on duty free purchases, thus curtailing this particular practice and bringing the return flight back to some degree of normality. Though I always thought it was very odd that the airlines would allow all these passengers on the flights with so much hand luggage any way, well above the published carry on limits, but I guess this is China! This would certainly never be allowed to happen in Europe, especially with the budget airlines, as they are incredibly strict with their hand luggage policy.

Another frustration of air travel in China, is that even when you are lucky enough to be travelling business class, often the business lounges are full to bursting, and many is the time I have wandered round unable to find a seat and just had to turn around and go back out to the main terminal and try my luck, and some of these lounges are huge. Just another example of the sheer volumes of people the air travel network has to try to cope with every day. But travel is always about timing. There was one memorable occasion when Julie and I decided to chance it and fly away for our vacation the day after Chinese New Year. I had some work commitments that prevented us leaving earlier, and it was normally our preference to get out a couple of days earlier than Chinese New Year to avoid the mass migration, so I hoped the day after Chinese New Year would be quieter. Imagine our surprise when we arrived at the airport and wandered to the lounge with our fingers-crossed. It was absolutely, 100% empty. We were the only 2 people in the airline lounge that day. So my tip for Chinese travel around Chinese New Year, wait until the day after the festival before heading out.

The first major challenge you will likely face after your flight, is when you finally emerge out through the arrivals doors. In the big city international airports of Shanghai Pudong and Beijing Capital, they are all waiting for you, the black cabs. Unlicensed taxis at airports are the first gauntlet you will have to run. It is quite shocking just how many there are lying in wait, all poised to grab those unsuspecting tourists, those first, confused timers to China. And they have all the tricks to suck you in. Those landing into China for the first time are always vulnerable, not knowing what to expect from the country, and a friendly smiling face is always going to be a welcome sight. There are plenty of black cab drivers who will approach you as you exit with your luggage, asking if you need a taxi. Just politely decline and keep on walking, otherwise it will cost you. A taxi trip into the centre of Shanghai should cost less than 200 RMB and usually less than 150 RMB. If you take a black cab, they will take you to your destination, but they will charge you whatever they think they can get away with, typically as much as 600 RMB. And not only that, you will know they are bogus because they will not drop you straight in front of your hotel, they will drop you around the corner, so you have to walk with your bags, because they don't want the concierge involved when you pay. Look, we all know the official taxis go to the official taxi stand, so just keep heading there, you will be safe there surely. I'm afraid not,

not in Beijing. At Beijing airport they are really in your face, the black cabs even park at the side of the official taxi rank and walk up to you as you're waiting in the official queue. None of the officials stop them. Even the official taxis can sometimes take you for a ride. They will lull you into a false sense of security, drive off and stop at the side of the highway just outside the airport to 'negotiate' the fare. What are you gonna do? No one is going to get out with all their luggage at the side of the highway in the middle of nowhere, especially if they have their family in tow. Another captive audience for the scumbags to prey off. Back in Shanghai Pudong, they have become a little more subtle in their methods. They have taken to working in teams, with young English speaking students to pal up with you. These youngsters are wearing suits, with airport badges on their lapels to look official, adding credibility to their offer of getting you a taxi. The most creative I have seen is these guys are now intermingled with all those officially hired personal drivers from companies and hotels, the ones that are waiting for their pick-ups holding a name on a board. The scammers don't know the names of course, but what they do is they hold an official looking board up which has all the logos of all the major Western hotel brands in the City printed on it, making it look like they are the official drivers for these hotels. These guys really have a lot of balls.

So if you find yourself landing in Shanghai Pudong and need to take a taxi, my advice is don't, just head for the Maglev instead. It is much cheaper, much faster and much safer. The Maglev (or magnetic levitation) is the fastest commercial high-speed electric train in the world and reaches over 400 km/h. It takes only 8 minutes to reach the Maglev station on the outskirts of the city centre. From there you can get on the Metro or get a taxi to your final destination, and you will be spared all the hassle of the black cab airport bullshit. If you find yourself landing in Beijing, God help you. Best to pay extra and arrange for a hotel car to pick you up. Arriving at other cities in China is not so bad, but you will still have unlicensed taxi drivers coming up to you, just not to the big city level.

I have learnt to avoid taxis to the airport at all costs in Shanghai. I have been involved in two accidents in taxis travelling from Shanghai city to Pudong airport. Thankfully I walked away from both with nothing more than a stiff neck, but still, the dangers are very real, and I have friends who ended up in hospital from similar situations in China. The problem is not so much in the city, as the speeds are lower, it's when the taxi gets onto the airport expressway, a straight road that runs for 20+ km all the way to the airport. Once on the expressway, some of the taxi drivers just go crazy, and this is when it can get scary and dangerous. With cars weaving in and out of lanes and with hesitant drivers who decide not to turn off at the last minute and swerve back onto the carriageway, it is a dangerous place. Hence the two accidents. Crawling out of a crumpled taxi in the middle of the highway and grabbing your luggage to flag down another cab is never going to be a highlight of anyone's trip. But I still keep doing it, every time I say never again, but there is always some situation I find myself in and just say 'oh well, just this once, I'll get a taxi'.

The last 'never again' moment for me was when I had finished meetings at one of our company's factories in Shanghai and they ordered me a taxi to take me back to the airport. The taxi came, it was much better than your average taxi, it even had rear seat belts, so I thought, okay. The drive through the city was okay, but the fun started when we got on to the expressway, though not for the reasons I outlined above. The problem was as soon as we got onto the expressway, the driver started falling asleep behind the wheel. I could see him through in his rear view mirror. The first couple of times he started dozing off and caught himself, as you do, snapping back to attention. But we have all been there as drivers, once this starts, it only gets worse. And every few moments he was micro sleeping and I had to start banging on the plastic panel between us to wake him up. So, we're travelling down the expressway at 80km/h with the driver napping off and the car starting to veer into the next lane, and I'm banging the panel and talking to him in Chinese all the way to try to bring him back to attention. A difficult decision, do I stop the cab and get out in the middle of nowhere, or do I try to keep him awake until we get to the airport, though there was still 20km to go. I took the latter choice and thankfully managed to keep the guy awake. Of course, as soon as we pulled into the airport he perked up. There is something about the straight long road that makes people drowsy, very dangerous. That was my last 'never again moment' and ever since then, I have never taken the taxi to the airport. I always get a cab to the Maglev station and take the expressway section by Maglev, much safer, more reliable and you get there in one piece.

I know I have had a bit of a bitch and a moan about air travel in China in this chapter, and it certainly has its own peculiarities, but we all know air travel can challenge everyone at times, no matter where in the world you are. Plus, reading about the times I have enjoyed smooth, comfortable and hassle free trips in China would not make for a particularly interesting or entertaining read. Having travelled regularly across all the industrialised regions of the world over many years, I feel I am in a pretty good position to contrast and compare travel experiences across the planet, and whilst my travels in China and across Asia have been punctuated with some very memorable and difficult events, overall, I would have to say that flying around Asia is still far better than the equivalent experience you get in the US. At least in Asia you are usually transiting through ultra-modern, brand new airports, and the lowest moments are normally just down to incompetence and lack of experience in the Asian staff. In the US they have no such excuses, and the low points of travel across the US are just down to bad attitudes, a unique 'don't give a shit' style of customer care, and ever more ludicrous cabin rules the airlines choose to put in place, all served against a backdrop of crumbling airports and antiquated infrastructure. But all those stories are for another time and another book.

Another thing you notice when flying around China, is that China loves land reclamation. Every time up take a flight that skirts the coast, you can see the slow process of land reclamation going on from the air. Huge rectangles marked out, projecting into the sea, in varying stages of being filled up with earth by a long slow column of trucks. Quarrying out mountains and filling in the sea. It's happening up and down the coast. Even the factory I moved to Dalian to build was on newly reclaimed land in an industrial zone an hour out of the city.

Even in just the 6 years I was living in Dalian, I watched the city expand its coast line through land reclamation in several locations around the greater metropolitan area. From our apartment window, we watched the city harbour area slowly extended into the water several hundred metres over the years. It was a real privilege to watch the premier city location emerge, as it slowly turned from a massive strip of dirt to a vibrant thriving new tourist district over that time. First was built a brand new international conference centre, an ultra-modern design that looked like a spaceship had landed. Next came hotels, shopping malls and kilometre upon kilometre of dozens of brand new high rise apartment blocks arranged into new neighbourhoods. Next came the extension to the metro to join this new district up with the city. And whilst all this was going on, the city was busy building another new tourist attraction on a massive scale. All along the coast, running the entire eight kilometre stretch, is now a European style city block, built in some of the most famous historical architectural styles. There are copies of grand Parisian apartment blocks, Milanese-style buildings, Swiss wooden chalets, a mini St Mark's square, a tower of Babel, and running through all of this is a copy of a Venetian canal, complete with gondola trips for the tourists. The whole thing may have a hint of twee-ness about it, but you cannot fail to be impressed with the unbelievable scale and vision of what they have done, and overall it is just such a fun place to wander around. There are always new cafes and restaurants opening in amongst this pseudo-city all the time. It truly has been inspirational to watch all of this rise from the new dirt of land reclamation over my 6 years there. It was a valuable lesson for me in just what can be achieved if you have vision. And the building work has not finished yet. They have already started work on a new cruise terminal, to position Dalian within the rising cruise industry in Asia, and the foundations have already been completed for an ultra-tall skyscraper, to be called the Dalian Greenland Center. At a planned 518m tall, once completed, this is due to be the 10th tallest building in the world when it opens. Someone really has big plans for the city of Dalian and is determined to put the 'city you have never heard of' on the world map.

All of this land reclamation does have consequences of course. One lesson I have learnt from watching this area being slowly built from my apartment window, is that you really need to be careful when buying coastal property in China, because in 5-10 years' time it is highly probable the city will have reclaimed more land, created a new coast further from your seaside property and built another row of high rise apartments in front of you, spoiling your view. So be warned. There are also always whispers about how the speed of construction is done at the expense of the quality of build, and plenty of my friends have said they would not consider buying any of the new build apartments, because they expect all the high rise blocks to start sinking in the future. So, a nice place to visit, but maybe you need to do your homework before considering buying in such an area. The seafront European style city is great for a weekend visit, but not really a place to live. I have seen evidence first hand of construction issues. After a year or so of completing the first phase of the pseudo European city, I was wandering around there one Sunday morning and the jogging path that runs between the buildings and the sea, running parallel to the sea front for 8 kilometres, had started to crack and split. Walking a little further, when I came across the first road between Phase 1 and Phase 2 of the building zones, perpendicular to the jogging path, this was cracked, splintered and buckled so badly, that huge holes had appeared that could swallow a person. It was like walking into a movie set about an earthquake. This was ultimately repaired over the months, but it does make you question what else is happening under the ground, and under the buildings, that you cannot obviously see. It will be very interesting to see what happens to this amazing development over the years. But unfortunately, this is typical of China. They have such huge vision, huge plans and you have to admire the way they just get on and do things, but there is always this underlying culture of cutting corners and saving a buck. I know, I have built a factory there, so I know how construction and contractors work. You really have to stay on top of these people to make sure quality is not compromised.

Another land reclamation question mark for the future in Dalian is the new airport they are building. The Dalian airport I used was still in the middle of the city, called Zhoushuizi airport. It was old by comparison with many of those in China, being mostly built in the 80s and 90s, but it was only 25 minutes from my apartment in the CBD and only 5 minutes from our old factory. Imagine, I could leave my apartment and be sitting at the departure gate waiting for my airplane within only 30 minutes, domestic and international. Where else on the planet can you say that? This saved me an enormous amount of time waiting around at airports over the years.

When Dalian airport was originally built, it was outside the city of course, but such has been the expansion of Chinese cities in the last 20 years that the city eventually engulfed the airport and it is now surrounded by residential land, with no more room for expansion. Hence the local government is now busy building a new airport, called Jinzhouwan, an hour out of the city. It is really interesting every time you take off from the current airport and bank over the coast. You get a great view of the man-made island being created to house the new airport. It is currently one massive pile of dirt, growing in the ocean, with a thin roadway servicing it from the mainland over which endless convoys of lorries trundle with more and more dirt. To those not involved in construction it just seems a massive unreachable task. They are literally moving mountains. But they are making progress, and over the months, I have seen the island grow and take shape. You can see now where the terminal is going and the area for the runway. Very impressive to be an aerial spectator over the years.

So I think you're getting the picture now, China loves its land reclamation. But at the level that I have seen this happening, I truly believe that if they carry on reclaiming land at this rate, they will fill up a corridor across the Pacific Ocean and join their country up with the United States in the next 100 years. Now that would change the world map.

And talking of the world map, politics and land reclamation, the most controversial land reclamation project of all that China is doing is in the South China Sea. The news media is awash these days with tales and speculation about how many of the islands in the South China Sea are being extended by land reclamation and converted into military bases, providing naval and air support facilities to give China a foot hold deep in the region. And this is despite their ownership being disputed by several countries in the region. The Chinese government really don't seem to care what other countries think. Sounds like the UK empire building of two hundred years ago and yet another example of China doing whatever they think is right for them and their country.

CHAPTER 9

STARING INTO THE ABYSS (OR TOILET TIME IN CHINA)

One of the most challenging parts of any Westerner's trip to China is the inevitable trip to the toilet. This can be a most enlightening and entertaining event. This is such an in your face (and up your nose) event that it features very highly in anyone's tales of their visits to China. It is certainly not possible to write a book about your experiences in China with confronting the whole toilet experience, so much so that it warrants a chapter on its own. I decided to place this chapter straight after the chapter on travel, because it's always during your travels around China when all those 'special' toilet incidents come. Enjoy.

The toilet challenge for Westerners in China revolves all around the need for squatting. Squat toilets are found in other parts of the world, in Mexico and parts of Southern Europe for instance, but the use of squat toilets in China is on such a widespread scale that try as you might you cannot avoid them forever. Even when there are Western style toilets available, many Chinese resort to squatting on them anyway, and it's pretty often you go in a cubicle only to find a pair of footprints on the toilet seat. Nice! There are even amusing signs appearing around modern public toilets in cities and airports, on the inside of the cubicle door, showing a red circle with a stylised picture of a man squatting on a toilet seat and a big red line across it – NO SQUATTING. Of course, they would have to actually close the door to see this, which many people don't do. Many is the time I have walked into a public toilet, only to be greeted by a row of happy smiling faces of guys squatting in the cubicles with their trollies round their ankles. Usually on the phone at the same time. Airports and shopping malls tend to have a mix of cubicle types now, some squats and some Western style sitting down jobs, so at least you get a choice, but the wait for sometimes the only sit down style can be painful.

Another very common sign in a Gents public toilet you see above the urinals says 向前一小步，文明一大步 (xiàngqián yi xiǎo bù, wénmíng yi dà bù), which literally translates as 'one small step forward, one big step for civilization'. This is essentially trying to emulate the famous Neil Armstrong moon landing phrase, so a better translation would be 'one small step for man, one giant leap for Chinese culture'. It's basically trying to get guys to stand closer to the urinal and stop them pissing on the floor. I know you ladies can have it tough as well, but for men, the toilet experience usually involves wading through half an inch of urine sloshing around the floor around the urinals. You really have to think if you want to keep your shoes after that or throw them away – gross. Sometimes you have to tip toe through the lake of piss holding your trouser bottoms up to stop them dangling too low and soaking up the yellow river. Whilst this is a scene not out of place at any low grade night club's pissoir anywhere in the world on a Saturday night, it's usually as a result of blocked plumbing rather than urinary misdirection. In China it just seems to be the norm, despite having an attendant employed to mop up the piss regularly, it just seems he can't mop it up fast enough. As soon as he's finished once round the floor, he's deluged with yet another tidal wave of wee, poor guy, what a job.

But the overflow of piss is not the only thing a toilet attendant has to contend with. There can also be an overflow in the shit department as well. In busy airports, you sometimes have to wait for a cubicle, especially if you want the sit down job rather than the squats. I once walked into one gents toilet in my local airport only to be met with the delightful sight of the toilet attendant squatting in the corner with his trousers and underwear round his ankles, and shitting into a plastic bag. All the cubicles were full and the guy obviously wasn't prepared to wait. I've seen some gross sights in my time, but this was definitely an eye-opener for me. And it wasn't just a plastic bag, it was one of those great big black plastic rubbish bags and it was already full of the brim with stuff he had picked up round the toilets. Each toilet attendant in China seems to have been issued with a massive pair of wooden tongs, about 3 feet long. Really useful for picking up all those used ass wipe papers that are strewn everywhere. There are usually many more shitty papers strewn around your average Chinese public toilet than a Westerner is used to, because they encourage the user not to flush the paper down the toilet. Instead they leave a little waste paper basket in the corner of each cubicle to dump your dump paper. And these always seem to be overflowing whenever I have to visit. Not a pleasant sight or smell. Hence the need for the attendant to be armed with his shitty stick, an absolute necessity if you ask me. So, the attendant was stooped over his massive bag of everyone's paper and shite he had collected, trying to add to the pile himself. He was happily squeezing and straining, whilst normal service went on around him. No one seemed to pay him any attention, no one seemed to act as if this whole thing wasn't just a normal everyday occurrence. Mind you, how are you supposed to react to some total stranger taking a dump in the corner of your public toilet? The guys in the room with me must have thought it was normal, because not one of them did what Chinese normally do when presented with something out of the ordinary. Not one of them got out their smartphone to start videoing the guy. So full marks to them for showing some restraint. Anyway, I didn't stop to witness the end of the process. I just finished my business and got out of there as fast as possible. I didn't fancy hanging around to see what he did with his even fuller bag of shit afterwards.

The guy squatting in the corner was not unfortunately an isolated incident for me. I did on a separate occasion observe an unusual twist on this story when I was visiting a trade show in Beijing, which took the whole shit overflow thing to new depths for me. I popped into the gents for a quick piddle, and I was standing at the urinal doing my stuff, when in wandered some shabbily dressed farmer type. What he was doing at a professional trade show I'm not sure. Knowing China he may have been the multi-billionaire owner of the exhibition hall, who knows? Anyway, the guy looked pretty out of place even in a public toilet. He seemed unsure of what to do and where to go. It was almost as if he had never seen any of the sanitary fittings before. And sure enough, he dropped his gear and proceeded to hitch himself up and sit on the urinal next to me, with his arse cheeks straddling the porcelain and started making all the signs of doing a poo. He was a pretty short guy, so his legs were dangling down either side of the urinal, and he seemed quite at home with his decision. After a few grunts and groans from him and with me shaking myself dry to try to make a rapid escape from the surreal incident, suddenly the lady toilet attendant appeared brandishing a mop and starting screaming at him in Chinese. She started beating the guy off the urinal with her wet mop. Well the guy was completely taken by surprise. He tried to defend himself and staggered off the urinal, but I guess it must be pretty difficult defending yourself from a savage mop lady when you're desperate for a poo and your trousers are stuck round your ankles. He kind of hopped around with one arm trying to defend himself from the mop and trying to pull his gear up with the other. I'm guessing his urge to crap disappeared pretty quickly when the mad mop lady started screaming at him and taking a swing. But anyway, he kind of hopped out of the toilets pretty sharpish, still completely bemused about what he'd done wrong, still struggling to pull up his pants. I guess his cheeks must have gone into ultra-clench the moment the lady appeared with her mop, making it even harder to get his pants back on. I guess it could have been worse for him, she could have been armed with the shitty wooden tongs. So he disappeared through the exit damn quickly, never to be seen again. The whole incident must have only lasted for less than a minute, but made an indelible impression on me.

One of the ways that living in China opens up your eyes is that you see people have a completely different take on things, approaching normal everyday things in entirely different ways. This challenges your whole perception of how you go through life yourself, challenges your perception of what is normal and makes you think again about the way things are done in the West. I have found this a truly mind expanding experience that you just couldn't get staying in your own home society, behaving to the cultural and societal norms of the community. I absolutely expected to hear different attitudes and opinions when I moved to China, but I never dreamed that it would also show me different ways of using everyday objects. The guy sitting on the urinal is a great example. You can kind of see the logic going on in his head. He obviously had never seen a urinal before, never encountered this situation before and just went with it. It was misguided logic for sure, quite where he expected his shit to go I'm not quite sure, but at least he had a go.

I saw a much better logical conclusion reached by another guy in another public toilet when presented with the problem of where to wash his hands. He seemed like another farmer type guy from the fields, so he was certainly familiar with the squat toilet thing, because that's where he was coming out from when I was walking in. He was holding his hands out in that way you do when you don't want to touch anything until you have washed them. You could see the logic puzzle playing out in his eyes. It was pretty quiet in the bathroom at this point, only me and him, so there were no real clues for him, no guys lined up at the urinals. So what did he do? He walked over to the urinals and proceeded to try and start washing his hands in the liquid in the base. I guess it smelled pretty antiseptic with one of those toilet cleaner tablets in the bottom. This was all pretty strange to behold, but you know, if you've never seen one before, I guess there is a sort of logic to it, a urinal is a little like a small sink. Anyway, this time, I was a gentleman and helped the guy out and showed him the real sinks and how to use them, so I did my public duty, problem solved for him and life lesson learned.

These are pretty funny stories to tell friends in a bar over a beer, but they are also great examples of how different people from different backgrounds and experience approach things differently. I thought there was only one possible way of using a urinal, but what do I know? I've just had my mind expanded by some uneducated farmer from the villages. I'm sure if I went to this guy's farm I wouldn't have a clue about how to do some of the stuff he takes for granted every day. Everything is about context. Though it has been difficult for me to look at a urinal in the same way ever since.

And why is it that when you go for a leak in a gents toilet in China, whenever another guy walks in, he always comes and stands right next to you? In Western society guys stand as far away as they can from each other, not wanting to crowd each other's personal ablution space. But the old Chinese guys love to come and stand right next to you at the urinals, or sit right next to you in a restaurant. I once had a guy come and sit right next to me whilst I was having my breakfast in a hotel. The breakfast area was pretty quiet, with loads of free tables, yet this guy came and plonked his breakfast right next to me and proceeded to slurp down his noodles. Is it just me? Do I have an old Chinese guy magnet on my head? The younger guys don't do this, it's always just the older guys, farmers from out of the sticks. They clearly have a very different behaviour code to us Westerners and to big city Chinese. I truly cannot figure it out.

Ladies have it equally as bad, so my wife tells me. Her stories of what she has found floating in and around the squats are toe curling. Used sanitary towels and period blood top the list, not to mention the shit daubed around the squat pan and I thought women couldn't miss in the loo, so why do they also have floods of piss everywhere?

But despite all the unsanitary squalor you have to endure, all that squatting in the toilet does have some real benefits, just think of all the time you save at the gym on leg workouts. I must have relatively weak glutes compared to the average Chinese because even I struggle to get up out of the toilet after a good squatting session. It's certainly not a relaxing experience if you're not comfortable with the whole thing. The Chinese seem to have no problem squatting anywhere, whether it's for their ablutions or just as an alternative to sitting around outside, they just seem to be comfortable squatting. If they're waiting at the side of the road for something, maybe to be picked up by a car or waiting for a bus, some of these people seem to prefer to squat rather than stand.

As part of the China versus the West mentality, the Chinese do have a paranoia about what Westerners think about them. I have it from the mouths of the folk themselves that there is a long held belief that all Westerners think Chinese are stupid, which surprised me, but that's what they think. I guess we all have our stereotypes to fight against. This paranoia was no better displayed for me than when I opened up one edition of China Daily one day. China Daily is an excellent English language newspaper in China that you find distributed free in airports, on airplanes, in coffee houses, etc., but totally state controlled of course. This particular edition featured a whole one page article (and it's a broadsheet so it was a big article) on why squatting for the toilet is better than sitting on a toilet seat like us Westerners. It expounded in tremendous detail all the health and hygiene advantages and benefits, and how superior it was culturally. Can you believe it? I just thought it was so funny and so unbelievably paranoid that the Chinese government feels the need to try and justify its toilet habits to the rest of the world.

Another toilet trend I have seen emerge in recent years is actually right out on the streets rather than in the WC. Most days walking round the city I would see at some point some mother pull down her young kid's trousers and let them wazz in the street, sure. But I started seeing a new twist on this. The mothers now clothe their little kids in trousers which are split right along the crotch. And I don't mean just a little slit. This is all the way up the front and all the way up the back. This tends to be for kids just starting to walk, up to 4 year olds. So now mothers don't need to drop their kids' kecks whenever they're desperate for a pee, they just get them to squat down in the street. The mothers will also sometimes pick the kids up and dangle them in mid-air, one hand under each leg, so we can all have a good look at the stream of piss as it flies through the air. And I mean anywhere on the street. I've seen it happen in the middle of the pavement, on the side in the gutter, I've seen a mother holding her kid over one of those public waste bins screwed to a lamp post, and that was for number 2s not just number 1s. I've even seen them let their kid just piss on the marble floor of a shopping mall, in the middle of the walkway. Can you believe it? I guess when you've got to go, you've got to go. What happened to the good old nappy? Why do they now have to let it fly anywhere and everywhere so we all have to be part of it? Are they just trying to save money? Are they lazy because they don't want to change a nappy? Is this yet another issue where they're trying to take the cultural high ground? What next, are we going to see another full page spread in China Daily explaining how nappies are the devil's handkerchief and that we should be teaching our kids to embrace their natural naturist selves by putting their wiener on show at every opportunity, so they can grow up to be better adjusted people at one with their minds and bodies? There are always two sides to everything, and you can certainly appreciate that reducing the use of nappies reduces landfill and sewage pipeline blockages, but if it's at the expense of rivers of kiddie piss running down our streets and shopping malls, I'm not sure that is really a step forward.

I know I have written a lot of toilet humour so far, but it is such a massive part of any Westerner's China experience. Though so far, I have only covered the more civilised end of things, the stuff you get to experience in big cities, in hotels, restaurants, shopping malls and at airports, just wait until you get out into the Chinese countryside and need the loo.

China has some amazing world class landmarks spread throughout the vast country. There is a never ending list of incredible natural landscapes to explore and enjoy. It really is such an important part of your time in China to make sure you get out of the big cities and go and see the unique natural beauty of China. But in doing this, as with any hike into the mountains anywhere in the world, you will inevitably hit the toilet challenge at some point. And China presents you with many weird and wonderful solutions to your plight.

One of the first times Julie and I took a drive out to a local mountain range for a bit of hiking, it was a wonderful spring day. We were out towards Lǚshùn, about an hour's drive west of Dalian. It was beautiful sunshine, but not too hot. Perfect for hiking, with a cool breeze once you got up high. After a few hours of following the trails up the mountain, we spotted a concrete shack at the side of the path, which was clearly put there to provide basic toilet amenities to hikers. Never one to miss an opportunity, we stopped for a quick pit stop. When you're out hiking with Mother Nature, you never know when the next man-made facilities will appear, before you have to resort to nipping behind a bush.

With the first tentative step inside, the ammonia hit you like an air bag. Progressing deeper required forcing your way through a thick steamy wall of ammonia, with every step causing your eyes and nose to run more and more as you penetrated further into the sanctum. In the man's side, the rough concrete trough that was meant to be a communal urinal was inches deep in all kinds of 'stuff' that I cannot begin to describe and that I had no intention of getting close enough to find out. It looked like what I imagine the sediment at the bottom of a cess pit to be, building up over years and years. I had no intention of adding to it. No problem I thought, I'll just use the toilet instead. If you've ever wondered what's it's like to take a dump balancing precariously on two thin concrete posts with your arse hanging out over a cliff, then I know just the place to recommend. Squelching round the corner to the cubicle, I discovered there was no toilet. Instead there was just a really big hole in the concrete floor. Straddling the hole were two concrete posts, each about the width of a human foot, fixed horizontally to the floor and reaching out across the gap where the floor should have been. I stared down into the abyss. The concrete shack had been cleverly built jutting out away from the edge of the hiking path, to the extent that the back wall actually stuck out over a sheer drop, a cliff with about a 100m drop straight down. This was the best thing I had ever seen to stop anyone from their urge to poop. I could not imagine anyone voluntarily dropping their trousers and straddling those concrete posts either side of such a sheer, vertical drop. And an obviously fatal one if you slipped and plummeted through the toilet floor, and what a way to go that would be. But I guess we have all experienced times when you absolutely, nothing in the world is gonna stop me, must go, and judging by the gungy residues on the concrete posts, it looked like some had tried. To top it all, there was no loo paper of course. Maybe you're just expected to shake yourself clean whilst dangling over the drop?

Getting loo paper in China is another learnt art form. Toilet paper must have some really valuable alternative use in China, since it is quite rare to find any in public toilets in China. I imagine there must be a network of black market, underground trading dens across the country, dealing in all those most rare of commodities in China; toilet paper, public bathroom soap, and the rear seat belts from taxis. If you want toilet paper in a public bathroom in China, you are supposed to pick it up as you walk in, before you get to the cubicles. There is usually a communal dispenser on the wall at the entrance to the cubicle section, and you just help yourself to some. But if you don't know this, and most foreign visitors don't of course, you usually find yourself a little stuck after doing your business. That's why very quickly in China you learn to carry around a packet of paper travel tissues in your pocket wherever you go.

Since that very first delightful encounter on the mountain, we have experienced many such concrete cess pits like this half way up mountains during our hiking trips. Though never again one with such innovative use of gravity as a replacement for plumbing. Maybe we just stumbled upon an unsuccessful prototype.

If you are looking for a real ethnic treat, then you should head out to the far West to hike into the rural landscape to experience 'real' China. There you may be lucky enough to experience the farmer's village style communal toilets, where you all get to hang your arses over a trough together and do what comes naturally, all in the playful atmosphere of being able to chat to your neighbour shiting next to you. And all in the fragrant open air, so you can wave at passers-by since there is no door or fence in front of the trough structure to hide your Western modesty. Always makes for a great family photo for your Instagram account.

CHAPTER 10

DANCING IN THE STREETS (OR FUN & GAMES IN CHINA)

Do you remember the old Martha and the Vandellas classic 'Dancing in the streets'? Or you may remember the great David Bowie and Mick Jagger version from the 80's? Either way, if you ever get to stroll through any Chinese city in the evening you will find them literally 'dancing in the streets'. It's called 'tiàowǔ guǎngchǎng', which means 'dancing in public squares'. This Chinese square dancing is generally a pastime of the older female generation, although occasionally you see a few people in the groups outside this demographic, including the occasional man. It's seen as a mixture of social and exercise for China's rapidly ageing society. The bigger the neighbourhood, the bigger the public space, the bigger will be the dance troupe in the evening. You see dancing every time you walk round any Chinese city, so I don't know if the same ladies go out every night or if more than one troupe shares the same public space such that they alternate. Some public squares are so big of course that they play host to several different dance troupes each evening.

These events get quite elaborate. Apart from all the choreography and teaching and practising the dances, there is usually a uniform to wear for the ladies. You can definitely spot a troupe as they all wear the same thing, so it's clearly very well organised. They will also be armed with large speakers to broadcast their music. This is especially necessary when these dance troupes have several hundred people per team. I imagine there is quite a prestige in being the dance leader or choreographer, giving someone real social standing in the neighbourhood.

Julie was out with friends one evening walking to a restaurant. There were a couple of visitors from the US with them, colleagues of one of her friends. As they were strolling to the restaurant through the city streets, they came upon one of these big dance troupes in action, in a large public square. One of the visitors said that they had always want to do that. Julie, never one for being shy, grabbed her by the hand and said, 'well you'll never have another chance like this'. So the group of foreign ladies all joined the back of the crowd and spent the next 20 minutes learning the dance routines and joining in, much to the amusement and joy of the locals. Julie told me her friend was so overjoyed to have done something like this, joining in real life on the streets, not just whizzing past things on the usual tourist escalator.

But as these outdoor dance activities have grown, so has the noise they create. Especially when there is more than one dance troupe competing for space and air time in the square. Inevitably this has led to noise complaints to people living in the area and there have been a growing number of noise pollution regulations imposed in Chinese cities, imposing heavy fines for disturbing public order after 9pm. This isn't a real problem to most Chinese as they seem to be tucked up in bed before this. That's another interesting thing about China, they start real early and finish real early. Try and find a restaurant open after 9pm, it can be pretty frustrating as a Westerner when you want a late night drink with friends. All pure Chinese restaurants and hotels are dead by 9pm, some even earlier. You need to know where the bars are that cater for the local foreign expat community, and these are only found in big cities. Many is the time I have been on business in some small Chinese cities, with nowhere to go once dinner is over by 8pm.

What I really admire about the Chinese square dancing, is not the fact that it brightens up any stroll around the city, but that it shows what a great sense of community the Chinese have in their cities. I cannot imagine such a thing happening in the West. In the UK, neighbours rarely speak to each other now, let alone spend any time together to get to know each other.

Whenever I host Chinese visitors in the UK for work, one thing they often say to me is how boring it is in the evening there, they say there is nothing to do. They are used to living in very vibrant city communities where people are out on the streets in the evenings, dancing, playing cards, in a place where all the shops are open and food stalls are spilling out onto the streets. In typical small town UK, everything closes after work, no one is on the streets, there is no sense of community and the place feels dead. Quite shocking to someone from Asia. A rise in violent crime is partly to blame, and has created a sense of fear on the streets in any UK city today, keeping people locked up in their homes every night sitting in front of the TV. It is easy as a foreigner to feel quite envious of the open and friendly street culture that the Chinese have developed.

Life in China seems somehow simpler, and people go about their lives with a more positive attitude and are less affected by what goes on around them. Sure, China has just as much crime on the streets, but the mood you soak up walking around any Chinese city is a bright and optimistic one, and as a foreigner it gives you a sense of peace and security. Yes, the police in China are well known to crack down heavily on anyone that steps too far out of line, but is this wrong, if it makes you feel safe? Every expat I have ever spoken to about this has said to me that they feel completely safe walking around a Chinese city at night. Can you say that about your town back home?

One good example I once saw first-hand of police heavy handedness was when I was attending a trade show in Beijing. I was walking round the booths when this guy shot past me, chased by a mob of policemen. It turns out the guy had stolen a laptop off one of the trade stands. Well they caught up with him pretty quick and immediately knocked him to the ground and started beating him all over with long wooden sticks. Pretty brutal behaviour to us sensitive foreigners. After they had given the guy a damn good pummelling, they then manhandled him onto a stool and wrapped the guy head to toe in sticky tape and cling film to fix him to the chair. I guess it saves money on handcuffs. This was basically a make shift holding pen whilst they waited for the police van to turn up. Despite the gruesome scenario, it was pretty funny seeing this thief covered completely in tape like a plastic wrapped mummy, stuck to his chair. This was definitely a real life example of rough justice. In the West I'm sure these police would get the book thrown at them, and end up in jail themselves for 'violating the suspects rights' and 'excessive use of force', but in China this is just how things are done. Judge, jury and dishing out the punishment all in one, all in real time. It sure must save on wasting public money on needless paperwork. If you step out of line you will get physically beaten. People understand that. That's their system.

When I moved to Dalian in 2011, I was told that they were still holding public executions of murderers, in the local football stadium. And again, in a symbolic gesture that saved public money, the family of the murderer was expected to pay for the bullet used to shoot the guy dead. I never got to see this spectacle, the practice stopped pretty soon after I arrived. I always wondered how they got the audience in. Public ballot? Free open door policy? Were you invited like a member of a jury? Were you expected to buy tickets? Was it considered a form of entertainment by the masses? Did they have hot dog stands at the venue? A weird concept for sure.

What's also weird is when the Chinese try their hand at Western and other non-Asian forms of entertainment. The Chinese Charlie Chaplin impersonator was certainly a strange but memorable one for me. I've seen a few Michael Jackson impersonators as well whilst in China, and these guys usually give it their all, though the Chinese belly dancer may have been the most odd. Chinese are just not cut out for belly dancing, for a start they have no belly, plus no ass and no boobs. I think the dancers were female, but I couldn't really be sure. You often get entertained with these kind of artistes at big conferences or business functions. I'd really rather they stick to Chinese art forms.

The Chinese art forms are great. I particularly like the Sichuan face changing entertainer. I remember the first time I saw one of these guys. The concept is simple enough and doesn't sound particularly entertaining, a guy has a series of masks and changes them quickly, all played out to a rousing traditional Chinese musical backdrop. It's an ancient art form from traditional Sichuan opera. But the sheer number of masks and the ultra-fast speed at which they change them, faster than the eye can follow, always leaves you wondering what the secret to the technique is. It is said to be a closely guarded secret. This is all so mesmerising for a Westerner because it is just so different. There is nothing like this in the West, and that's what us foreigners hunger for, that's why we moved to China, we are looking for new and astounding experiences, and for me, the Sichuan face changer epitomises all that is strange and wondrous about living in China.

Another fine Chinese traditional pastime is mahjong, a board game that seems at first very confusing, with lots of tiles in play at one time, the tiles having only Chinese characters on. There are 144 tiles in total, and four players, so there is a lot going on during a game. Julie got into this game big time because when we arrived, there was an ongoing wives club weekly mahjong morning. The lady that hosted taught Julie the intricacies of the game and she quickly picked it up. Julie brought more friends into the weekly play and it grew into quite a crowd. What a great thing to become involved in as expats, a uniquely Chinese experience. In the West it is not easy to buy a mahjong set, let alone find someone to play it with. Over the years, the venues moved around between different people's apartments and occasionally they even took their games outside. One memorable occasion was when the ladies took their mahjong sets out to a local park during cherry blossom season. There they were, with ladies from all over the world, Spanish, Indian, British, and Brazilian, playing this traditionally Chinese game and enjoying the glorious weather. They became quite a spectacle, with groups of Chinese locals stood around smiling in disbelief at all these foreigners playing their game and obviously enjoying it so much. Julie said to me 'they were all smiling as if they wanted to join in with us, some did help us out, and we loved it, a truly unforgettable experience'.

Julie said that learning the game was a bit of a challenge for some people, particularly when they had just arrived and had no Chinese language to fall back on. The tiles were helpful for them as a basic learning aid for a few of the characters, but still, new ladies had to struggle over the language barrier to play. Julie told me 'in their enthusiasm, some ladies would still shout out "snap" instead of 'mahjong' when they'd won, so funny'. Some of the pain was alleviated a little when they discovered the automatic mahjong table that the Shangri-La Residences had fitted into a special mahjong room for the residents. An auto table does all the shuffling and dealing out of the tiles for you, really helpful and fun to watch if you haven't seen one before.

The weekly mahjong sessions eventually settled at a permanent venue, and Friday mornings became mahjong at Café Copenhagen for so many of the wives expat circle. Café Copenhagen is a Danish style café, with foreign owners and an English speaking serving team. The local Chinese manager Tony was a really helpful and cheerful guy and used to spoil the ladies with free cake. Expat life by its nature involves people coming for fixed term contracts, so typically friends would arrive, be assimilated into the group and then leave within the space of two to three years. So there was a regular churn amongst the group's numbers. But Café Copenhagen became a focal point for so many expat activities, not just mahjong. The Friday morning mahjong sessions continued for several years, and Julie was there right up until her last session on the day before we left Dalian for good. It was a sad thing for Julie to leave her favourite pastime. These events gave so much pleasure to so many people over the years. But Julie had taught several newcomers well and so could pass on the torch to the next generation of expat wives.

One of the big Asian pastimes that most Westerners really dread is KTV or Karaoke, and I was no different when we moved to China. In all my previous business trips there, I counted myself lucky that I had avoided the perils of karaoke up to that point, but I guess it was only a matter of time. And sure enough, a few months after we arrived, I was on a business trip down near Nanjing with a bunch of colleagues and our local team. It was a very boozy night and of course the locals ended up taking us to a karaoke place. When you still have a fear of karaoke, travelling there for the first time really makes you sober up. You have to think hard to prepare, what are you going to sing? How will you perform? Will I make a tit of myself? A very scary feeling when it's something you have never done before. The whole party had been drinking a lot already that evening, so the mood was really upbeat as we headed to KTV on a bus together. I remember the first time walking into our karaoke room at the venue, like a small nightclub without people, like one that hadn't opened yet, but once your party piles in, things fire up very quickly. The karaoke veterans kick the evening off and the fun is away. When it came to my turn I decided to sing Adele, Rolling in the Deep, which was very popular at the time in China. It's a difficult song to sing but I have to say I sang it pretty well. So all in all, my first karaoke was a very positive experience. We all headed back to the hotel and carried on drinking mojitos until 2am. I had no meetings the next day, and just was just travelling home, but I remember getting up and standing in the shower at 7am, staring down at the bottom of the shower cubicle, everything spinning, thinking 'I'm still drunk'. I then had to endure a car journey to the airport and a snooze on the flight back to Dalian. And I remember getting picked up by my driver at the airport and I was still drunk even then.

Since then, I have enjoyed far too many karaoke nights, probably hundreds by now, so I have honed my craft and learnt more than a few things about the whole process. I learnt that there are two basic styles of karaoke, one where you book a private room for just your own group, so you are singing only in front of your friends, and another where it is an open bar and you sing in front of strangers in the whole bar. The private room version is the most common type in China, and some KTV venues are so big that they have dozens of such rooms, in all shapes and sizes. The second style is generally the type you find in Japan, so I call this Japanese style. You also find a mixture of both styles all over Asia, including Korea and Singapore. When it comes to karaoke, the Koreans are the most serious of all. They even have karaoke places there, where people go to practice first, before they go to the main karaoke bar later in the evening.

I also learnt that all that anxiety you feel before you first go to karaoke is all unnecessary, because basically you are there to make a fool of yourself in front of a bunch of drunken friends. No one cares if you're good or bad, it's not an audition for X Factor, no one is judging you, everyone is just there to have a good time. No one is particularly listening to you and no one cares or even particularly remembers what you did the next day. It's essentially a party, and I think that's the appeal and the cleverness of the karaoke experience. The music, singing and drinks help you and your friends create a party atmosphere immediately. But I also learnt that once you start down the karaoke road, it is difficult to stop. Julie and I always have such a good time there that we can't wait to go again and again and again. But it can be difficult for the night to end when everyone is having such a good time, particularly if there is no work the next day. Many is the time we have been singing until 3 or 4 in the morning and much longer on some occasions.

There was one particular place we always went in Dalian, called KTV Party, in the centre of Min Zhu Guang Chang, the nightclub area of the city. This was a huge multi-story building with dozens of karaoke rooms. The first time we pulled an all-nighter at the karaoke bar, I thought that it stayed open 24 hours a day, but we only found out that it didn't when they turned off the electricity at 6am in the morning. Stumbling out, blinking into the first light of day, and heading for breakfast at McDonalds became a frequent occurrence at the weekend.

I also learnt that if you want to sing well, you need to find songs that suit your voice, you just can't sing anything. The whole set up and acoustics of the room already help you a lot, with great reverb to make your voice sound much fuller than it really is, but you have to go through a few attempts until you find the song that really suits your voice. But once you do, suddenly you have your 'go to' karaoke song. You have then arrived and become an official Karaoke veteran.

By years 2 and 3, it got to the point that we were going to karaoke so often that I began to recognise the different models of the karaoke machines in the KTV bars, so I got to learn the different controls and knew what Western songs they would and wouldn't have listed on each type. It seemed that there were a limited number of models that had cornered the market, so 90% of the places we went would always have one of no more than 4 different models. Using the controls is a challenge at first, because they are all in Chinese. You can normally switch them to the English language, but obviously you need to know enough Chinese to know which buttons to press to change it, or get a Chinese friend to do it first, but after I had been learning Chinese long enough, I could find my way around the systems okay.

So why is it that karaoke has not caught on in the West? Sure, you can find karaoke bars in most Western cities, but you have to look hard. And whenever I have been in Western Karaoke bars (and I've been in a lot since leaving China), people are generally having a great time, so why is it not as popular as in China and across Asia? Karaoke seems a natural extension of a great evening out, after the restaurant, after all the drinking, what better way to carry on the good time. By then, people are ready for letting go a bit, for dancing and singing, loud music and lights. Are Asian people just more outgoing than Westerners? I don't believe so, and in some respects, I would say the opposite is true. Do they love music more than Westerners? I've never seen any evidence for this, Canto-pop and K-pop are massive in China, but no more popular than Pop and Rock in the West.

One key reason I believe that karaoke is yet to take the West by storm is due to a significant cultural difference in the relationships people have with their co-workers. In the West, it is not so common to socialise regularly with your co-workers, but in Asia, it is very common for co-workers to go straight from work to a bar and hang out together. When I lived and worked in the UK, the only occasion I would get together with my co-workers after hours was for business dinners, to entertain visitors and once a year for a company Christmas party. I always thought it a shame that we didn't spend more time together, and just accepted that that was the cultural norm at the time and I just thought, well people have their own life. As I got higher in the company, we would have the occasional Board dinner together, and on very rare occasions we would have the wives over as well, but this didn't happen until I'd known and worked with people for 15 years or more. When I moved to China, straight away Julie was there socialising alongside my co-workers and we got to meet their spouses and families as part of after work dinners. I found that business in China is a much more family oriented affair and is much more about building deeper relationships on a personal level with your co-workers. And I have to say, I discovered to my surprise, that I much preferred this style. It helped you understand and relate to your colleagues much better when you knew their home life, their spouses, and their children and made for a more intimate style of business. When I moved back to the West, I found things were getting better slowly, with modern management styles that encourage leaders to spend more personal quality time with their team, but despite this, the business of doing business is still quite a direct and mechanistic process there, rather than the fluid and empathy driven practices in China and across Asia. Once I returned to Europe, I deliberately took the Chinese style of business relationship building back with me, and regularly take co-workers and their spouses out for dinner now, along with my wife. Above all, it's just fun, so why not.

Another significant barrier to karaoke not yet attaining the same level of popularity in the West as it enjoys in the East is the cost. A night out at a karaoke bar in the US, by the time you've covered the room hire and all the drinks, and paid the 20% tip, can easily rack up 100 US dollars an hour, even for a small crowd. In China, this would cost only one tenth of that price. There were many times in China when I went to pay for the evening's entertainment at the end of the night and had to do a double take on the bill, it just seemed far too cheap. A think there is also an issue in the West that karaoke bars are predominately of the Japanese, open bar style, which tend to be a bigger source of embarrassment for anyone not used to getting up on stage in front of a bunch of strangers. I would love to see more karaoke bars in the West, it would certainly extend my night out choices, but until these barriers are overcome it's going to be a long time coming.

The rise of the smartphone has made an undeniable difference to everyone's life. The services it allows access to expand all the time and the access to information it opens up no matter where you are is just incredible. But it also has a lot to answer for. Everyone has become addicted to their phone, and it is difficult for many of us to put it down, even for one minute, and I am as guilty of this as anyone. There are even recognised smartphone related phobias amongst people now, like the fear of losing a signal, called nomophobia, short for 'no-mobile-phone phobia'. A visit to any restaurant, and a trip on any public transport the world over is just full of people staring down into their smartphones. It is incredibly difficult for people to disconnect from the digital world these days and re-engage with the physical world and with real people. There is no clearer way in which the smartphone has affected behaviour than with the ability to take photos. Now everyone is a photographer, and the Chinese in particular have taken this to heart. Social media forces millions to try to outdo each other with photos taken at ever more exotic places and in ever more extreme locations. There are incredible statistics floating around about how more and more digital photos are being taken each year, with last year toping over 1 trillion. All down to the smartphone and the improvement in digital picture quality that has been achieved during this last decade. And the need for more and more computer chip memory is accelerating exponentially, with chip companies investing billions in new manufacturing capacity around the world. Dalian in particular has a huge Intel factory that has been through 3 phases of expansion already, just for making memory chips.

The Chinese love their selfies, and every time you step out and travel anywhere, you will always see people stopping and taking photographs of themselves. But the etiquette in China for photo taking has developed its own weird direction. Not content with just standing and having their photo taken in front of some nice landscape or interesting building, a strange series of poses, gestures and actions have built up to try to enhance the pose. The classic one is when girls raise their arms up in the air and fold them round to make the shape of a heart above them, often also done with two girls leaning into each other with their arms making the shape of a heart in the air between them. A simpler version of this is that people will raise their thumb and forefinger at an angle to each other to form the shape of a small heart. Another classic is when someone, or a small group of people, will jump in the air all at the same time to try and get a photo of themselves all in mid-air. My particular favourite is the one where ladies will hold up a long silk scarf behind them so it trails in the wind to get a really dramatic pose. But I never see such weird poses in the West. I am certainly impressed by the creativity of the Chinese to have dreamt up these things, but these behaviours have become truly obsessive now, you see them everywhere, and the need to constantly post new photos has caused some people to become extremely self-obsessed.

On WeChat, people can post photos to their contacts in a section called Moments, each Moment holds a maximum of 9 photos. It's similar to Facebook and is a great feature to keep track of friends and what they're up to, but it has also been hijacked by all these self-obsessed people. Some friends' WeChat moments are just endless pictures of themselves. Some of Julie's Asian girl friends are particularly self-obsessed. They will post 9 photos of themselves standing on a lawn or making a cup of tea, all with nothing but themselves in the photos. And they post these things every day, daily montages of photos of themselves doing the most uninspiring and mundane things. Why do they think people want to see that? Even when these people do go on vacation and have something interesting to photograph, they still make themselves the focal point of the photograph. I saw a photo from one self-obsessed selfie junkie stood in Paris, but completely obscuring the Eiffel tower behind them. They are obviously not even looking at the backdrop behind them, their eyes are completely focussed on themselves. Even the never-ending photos of food that we all have to obsessively post are more interesting. It can certainly be fun looking at photos of where friends have travelled, it helps to keep in touch with their lives, it's nice to know they are having a good time and can be a source of inspiration for your own vacation choices. But this constant stream of self-obsessed mediocrity is just a waste of pixels. These people seem to behave like they are media celebrities and seem genuinely wrapped up in their own self-delusion. I would suggest a trip to a therapist.

For inspiring and beautiful photos, Dalian is a great place, with its wide variety of coastal landscapes, its lakes and mountains, its unique architectural heritage and its seaside resort atmosphere. Lots to see and do for visitors. Dalian is known as the 'City of Romance', and one particular subset of visitors come specifically to take their wedding photos. Wedding photos are normally done six or more months before the wedding event, and are big business in China. There are numerous spots around the city where you will always see couples queuing up for their turn to have their 'unique' romantic shot. I'm sure the photos are amazing but the reality is far from that of course. It is quite amusing walking past these queues of young couples. Each has a crew of three people with them from their wedding company, a photographer, photographer's assistant and a costume assistant. So it can be quite a crowd if there are half a dozen couples in line. The couples are often dressed in ill-fitting off the rack suits and dresses, usually with the back of the bride's dress pinned up to force it to fit okay. And the brides-to-be are usually wearing athletic shoes underneath their dresses. I guess it's a long uncomfortable day for them as they have many sites to get to.

The most popular wedding photo spot nearest to our apartment was down the end of our road at Zhong Shan square, a large open green space surrounded by Russian imperialist style buildings. Sat in one corner of the square, the front steps of my bank, ICBC, has a very grand entrance and makes for a very impressive photo backdrop, so always attracts a queue of bridal couples. Driving around the city you quickly noticed the other key hot spots for wedding photos due to the crowds of wedding photo parties; at the harbour, on Bīnhǎi Lù (the coast road), at Xīnghǎi Square, plus a host of other coastal and beach beauty spots. The wedding photo trade quietens down for three months over the winter, but the rest of the year there is a steady stream of couples and I have never gone out into the city without seeing wedding photos being taken somewhere.

CHAPTER 11

I NEVER DID GET THAT HEAD MASSAGE (OR HEALTH & FITNESS IN CHINA)

Massage is a very popular way of relaxing in China and across Asia. But there are many types of massage experience. As an uptight Westerner, and worse than that, a stiff Brit, I am very uncomfortable with the whole idea of some stranger rubbing me all over. I have friends who go to massage regularly and find it a very relaxing experience, but I probably go about once every 5 years, and then whilst it's happening I am always just waiting for it to end.

Massage can be incredibly cheap in China, and I guess that's one of the reasons it's so popular. Most Westerners' first experience of massage in China is the foot massage. Not too intrusive, things can't get too intimate with that one surely. And usually you are dragged there by work colleagues late in the evening after dinner and drinking. So you're one of the work crowd and you just have to go along with it now. I was with a group of colleagues in Shanghai one evening and we all ended up at a foot massage place. There were about 10 or 12 of us, and a mixed group, so we were quite a large party to accommodate, but we found this place and everyone managed to grab a seat and there were enough girls around to start working on everyone's feet. All very relaxing and it even started to help subdue the more boisterous of our crowd, still high from the evening's drinking. Well, all this fell apart when one of the massage girls bent over and let rip a massive fart. The whole room just erupted with laughter. She went bright red and ran off into the back of the store. Poor girl. It was difficult for anyone to stay relaxed and focused after that.

Another foot massage I had was in Yixing, a small city two hours west of Shanghai, with 2 work colleagues. Our local host was the famous 'papa', our joint venture partner. A massive drinker, so a night out with him was always a mega-challenge anyway. We had our foot massages, it took around 40 minutes. My girl was a bit heavy handed, but that was okay. But at the end she invited me to go with her into a separate room to have a 'head' massage. I was a bit taken aback and politely declined, though she was never really clear about which 'head' she was offering to massage!

Another massage experience I had was when Julie and I were on vacation in some fancy Chinese beach resort in Sanya. Sanya is one of the top beach destinations in China, being the most southerly point of the country, and hence the only one you can seriously go to over winter to get some sun. The spa was heavily advertised, and you know what it's like when you're on holiday, you just come up with these stupid ideas to make the most of the resort. Let's go and have a spa day! So we went and had our treatments and it came to the massage, Julie had booked some all over body thing. I'd looked through the massage menu and went straight for the sports massage section, surely that's the manly thing to do, or so I thought. I opted for a deep tissue massage. A mistake on a couple of fronts. The first one was unbeknownst to me this involved massaging the buttocks. So when my towel came down and my masseuse started working on my ass, I went straight into tense mode, particularly as my wife was sitting next to me watching, as she hadn't left for her treatments yet. That was mildly uncomfortable enough, but the real discomfort came when the masseuse started to do the actual 'Deep Tissue' bit of the deep tissue massage. I am so naïve! It means exactly what it says. The girl gets her forearms and elbows and pushes hard into your legs and arm muscles, pushing right between the muscles, deep down to the bone and then scrapes her arm down your calf muscles or arm muscles. Wow, so painful. I thought they only did that in torture scenes in movies. I didn't realise you could pay to have it done to you. OMG, never, never again. Please guys, learn from me. Deep tissue massage is not a manly thing. I was whimpering like a little girl the whole time.

In the end, Julie & I found a great compromise with the whole uptight massage taboo thing. We bought a massage chair. What a great purchase. Now I can enjoy a relaxing massage without having a real person touching me. So now I'm on it almost every day. I have finally found the secret to a good massage, just hire a robot.

Whilst massage can be incredibly cheap, healthcare can be incredibly expensive. If you just want to go to the local hospital and line up for hours, sure it's cheap. But if you do go, it's like being a widget on a production line. You are just another piece of meat with a problem. And of course, they have a broader array of treatments to throw at you, because they practice Chinese medicine in hospitals, not just Western style medicine. There is also a big medical culture of putting people on a drip for everything in China. They don't prescribe many pills, if you have a cough or a cold, they send you to a massive hall to be plugged into a drip with hundreds of other people. That's how they prefer to administer their medicines. And when it comes to Chinese medicine, it can be quiet an eye opener when they start getting their acupuncture needles out. I personally have experienced the joys of cupping (pretty painful, and leaves you with a sore, scarlet red pattern on your skin for days) for a torn ligament in my shoulder (from too much bench pressing in the gym) and moxybustion (a form of acupuncture where they burn herbs on top of the needle to get heat into the body) for a painful knee.

With acupuncture and moxybustion, it's one of those situations where they say 'this won't hurt a bit' and sure enough it doesn't hurt at all when they put the needles in, no problem. But what they don't mention is that they don't stop fiddling with the needles once they're in, and that can be strangely uncomfortable. The doctor will periodically come and tweak or rotate the needle. I don't know why, perhaps to try to stimulate the area more, or perhaps they're bored. Either way, the needle can be pretty deep and depending on where the needle is located, when they twiddle it, it can be an unusually sickening experience, not always painful, just weird, like it is sparking off pain receptors that you have never experienced before and your brain just doesn't know how to cope with the feelings. The whole process of acupuncture and moxybustion is supposed to work by rebalancing the energy (or chi) flow in your body. Whilst some consider this all mumbo jumbo, what I see, having experienced it first-hand, is that the needles are likely stimulating your body to heal itself by triggering blood flow and stimulating the body's own natural defences, painkillers and healing mechanisms. It seems pretty logical to me, not a million miles away from electrostimulation or shortwave therapy to heal damaged muscles and tendons, just a different form of stimulus. Moxybustion adds an extra dimension to the unsettling feelings you can experience, because they keep burning the herbs on the end of the acupuncture needles, and keep relighting them when they go out. If they're using a lighter and playing the flame on the metal needle, guess what happens? Yes, it gets pretty hot down the needle, travelling right deep under your skin, like a soldering iron has been inserted into you. Not a nice feeling.

Turns out I had a torn meniscus for the Moxybustion treatment. Who's to say these treatments did or didn't help? No idea, they relieved the symptoms a bit I guess, but I still have that torn meniscus. I am a bit sceptical like most Westerners of these forms of what are considered 'alternative therapies' in the West, but I certainly didn't mind trying them out. I was opened minded about their benefits until I'd tried them for myself and to me it was really part of the expat experience to say that you had tried these things out. As an expat, you tend to have medical insurance from your company to cover all this, but many companies can get a bit twitchy if you write down acupuncture or similar Chinese treatments on the claim firm, so Chinese hospitals usually just write 'physiotherapy' on the form to get around it.

On another occasion when I was still having a few twinges from my shoulder, my wife persuaded me to go for a massage at her beauty place next door to our residences. I didn't particularly want to go but I thought I'd give it a go and she was very insistent, so I went and the lady asked if I was having any particular problems and I told her about the twinge in my shoulder. I soon realised my mistake when she proceeded to give me the massage from hell. After all the normal preliminary stuff, she got out a sharp stone and kept scrapping my bad shoulder really roughly, again and again. It was just like what they do when they want to scrape the skin off animal fur to make a pelt. It was the kind of massage where you are biting the pillow from the pain. And being a stiff upper lipped Brit I just stupidly kept my mouth shut and let her do it. Afterwards, once the bruising had really had time to develop, it looked like I'd been repeatedly slashed on my back in a knife fight. Why oh why do we do these things! Never again!

To service the wealthy expat community and growing middles classes, a massive international level healthcare industry has grown up in China and right across Asia. So if you want private healthcare with western trained doctors that speak a little English, it is all available, but you are going to pay massively for it.

You also have the same local vs international choice to make when it comes to dentistry. In our early Dalian days, a friend took us to a local dental hospital for a check-up and the lady that did me was extremely efficient and just got stuck into things. I hadn't been for quite some time so unfortunately I needed several small fillings. After on hour the lady dentist stopped working and asked me to come back tomorrow. But she'd left me with a big hole in my front tooth! I had to insist on her carrying on and completing the job. Going to a local Chinese dentist can be like taking your car to a mechanic.

We were fortunate to have a small branch of the big city private hospital right next door to our residences. Really convenient for seeing the doctor, but it also had a dentist. He was a nice enough guy, but he went all gooey every time my wife was there. He was obviously in love with her. The guy was okay for basic stuff like tooth cleaning and check-ups, but if you wanted anything major doing, he became very nervous, very quickly. My wife needed an emergency extraction of a major molar, and we managed to get an appointment at short notice with this guy next door. My wife sat down in the dentist's chair and the guy started to make all the preparations for the extraction, but he was obviously nervous, getting fidgety and sweating, He even started doing stretching exercises to limber up for the ordeal of getting the tooth out, extending his arms and stretching his fingers back. He was making us all very nervous, and all this time Julie was sat in the chair in obvious discomfort and getting more and more nervous. At some point we looked at each other and just got the same vibe to bail out. This was obviously not going to end well, so we just left and made our excuses. The dentist was obviously very relieved. It was clear he had never done anything like this before. So we were stuck with finding somewhere that could do a major piece of dental work at short notice. I started searching around on the internet for suitable international medical facilities locally, in Beijing, in Shanghai, in Seoul, in Hong Kong. But the problem for the Chinese places was that we couldn't get an appointment quickly enough, and for places further afield it was getting close to Christmas time, and some dentists were already on vacation. Eventually I found the Raffles Hospital in Singapore, a place we knew well and trusted to have good international standards. So I booked Julie in for her tooth extraction the day after next and proceeded to make our travel plans to travel the 4,500km to Singapore. A long way to go for the dentist, but needs must.

We eventually got to the Raffles hospital on time, a long painful journey for Julie, and we were introduced to Julie's dentist, a Californian called Emmanuel Taylor. He was a real expert at pulling teeth. You felt in very safe hands with

Emmanuel. The extraction was a breeze, but because it was a major molar, she was advised to have an implant, as it was a tooth you would definitely miss otherwise. She agreed to go ahead with it, and that's when I discovered that having an implant is a bit like DIY, as it involves a great big drill and lots of banging. Julie was hanging almost upside down in the dentist's operating chair to get the right angle for drilling into the jaw. Lots of blood involved in that one, which meant no flying the next day. So we got stuck in Singapore whilst she recovered over Christmas and couldn't meet out daughter in Shanghai for Christmas Dinner. Julie's Christmas dinner was mushroom soup, as that was all she could manage with her swollen face. So that was the story of how our local dentist ended up being in Singapore, 4,500km away from our home in Dalian. Dentists are like plumbers, once you find a good one you want to stick with them all the time. I travelled frequently to Singapore on business, so we had plenty of opportunity to go there if we needed treatment, but it was ultimately an expensive visit to the dentist.

I also had the pleasure of Emmanuel's personal expertise a year or so later. I was in Singapore for a few days on business, The first day of the meetings I felt an increasing ache in one of my wisdom teeth, so much so that I realised I would not last out the rest of the meeting days and keep my mind on the job, so arranged an emergency appointment with my favourite tooth puller the next day. Just a simple wisdom tooth extraction, right at the back, so no implant required for me fortunately. Although he did say he was surprised I still had all my wisdom teeth 'at my age', nice one. He had me back at the meeting that same afternoon, fantastic service. The moral of this dental story? Make sure you have a reliable support structure wherever you travel.

As an expat, whilst your expensive medical insurance might get you into any number of high end overpriced private hospitals and clinics, that is all very well when you have time to plan and make an appointment. But in everyone's life there will always be those emergency incidents that force you into any local medical facility that you can find. I experienced just such an occasion one memorable night in Shanghai whilst I was out having dinner with my daughter, Heather. By this point, she had followed me out to China and was working as in English teacher in Shanghai. It was my birthday that evening and I was in the city over the weekend for business, so we met for a little father-daughter catch up time. We met right in the heart of the city, in amongst the bright lights and ultra-tall skyscrapers of Pudong, in LiuJiaZui. We dined at a wonderful Italian restaurant in the upmarket IFC Mall, on a terrace overlooking the Jin Mao, Pearl and World Financial Centre towers, always a stunning evening backdrop. My daughter has a severe peanut allergy, so is always very careful when eating out. The dinner was fine, and afterwards we strolled around the mall and Heather decided to stop and buy an ice cream. That was when things started to turn sour. After a few minutes of eating her ice cream she started feeling a tingling around her lips, which is her alarm bell for the fact that she's eaten some peanut. There must have been something in the ice cream. I had never seen her have an allergic reaction before, and I only knew what she had told me about it, so this was all new territory to me. She has to get to a hospital for a shot of adrenaline within 45 minutes or she can start slipping into a coma. She had told me that she carries an epipen to give herself valuable extra time, but on this occasion, when she needed it, she decided to come clean and tell me that she stopped carrying it around in China because she can't get a replacement if she uses it, oh fabulous. So what now?

Heather started to feel faint and I had to hold her up as she was starting to pass out. I dragged her around to the sidewalk to flag down a taxi and find a hospital, but this is one of the busiest tourist spots on the planet, lots of taxis whizzing past, but all full and no one would stop. So I needed a Plan B. We were pretty close to the Shangri-La Pudong hotel, so I dragged her over there to the concierge and explained our emergency and that I needed the nearest hospital urgently. He called a taxi, but of course it still took 20 minutes with all the traffic. But 'Thank God' for the Shangri-La, they may have saved Heather's life that night. The taxi took us to the emergency department of the Shanghai East Medical Centre, another 15 minute drive out of the city centre, in what seemed like a very quiet and dirty neighbourhood of apartment blocks, at least it seemed like that after all the bright lights and glitz of where we had come from. By this time, Heather could hardly get out of the taxi, such was the depth of her allergic reaction. I had to carry her through the double doors of the emergency department and manhandle her to the desk. Precious minutes were disappearing fast, the 45 minute window was already long up by then. Of course this was a Chinese hospital, so even at this time of night the A&E area was packed full of people, but Heather needed treatment right away. I used the finest Chinese I could muster to the guy behind the desk, 'huāshēng guòmǐn, huāshēng guòmǐn' I shouted, 'Peanut Allergy'. And in the finest tradition of the Chinese he just looked at me blankly with a 'didn't give a shit' expression. I repeated myself several times until I got a response. He responded in English, 'you need the International Hospital'. What? Where is that? Thinking we were in for another difficult taxi journey. '15th Floor' he told me. Okay, in the same building not so bad, things may be looking up. So we staggered down the corridor to the elevator, I was carrying her by then, and finally got in. Up we went to the 15th Floor. The doors opened and we stumbled out into the corridor. I looked right, I looked left. Everything was dark, no lights on either side, Oh Shit! What now? I started calling out for someone, 'Hello, anybody there?' I made a decision and headed left, dragging Heather along with me. She was passed out by this stage. I kicked open the double doors and pulled her through. Suddenly, one by one, all the overhead corridor lights came on in sequence in front of us, a couple of ladies emerged from a side door and came over and they escorted Heather to a treatment room. An Indian doctor turned up and within five minutes Heather was on a hospital bed with a drip in her arm and a shot of adrenaline in her blood stream. She improved tremendously quickly after that. Within minutes she was coherent and awake again. We had to stay there for another 3 hours until the doctor was satisfied she had stabilised well enough and we finally got back to her apartment at 3am in the morning. What a night, what an experience, what an unforgettable birthday.

When it comes to health, there is no better way of keeping healthy than with sports and other fitness pastimes, and China has many options to choose from. In Chapter 10, I explained about the street dancing, where you often see lots of ladies, and a few occasional men, dancing in the city squares and plazas in the evening in large organised groups. A stroll through any large city park will reveal lots of people out having fun and exercising, especially at the weekends. There are groups of guys sitting around smoking and playing cards and mahjong, or at least it's always men whenever I see them. I'm sure ladies play as well, but they must do it indoors.

One great eye opening pastime with a bit of exercise

thrown in is whip cracking (yes, you read that right). I don't know what has inspired these guys, and again I've only seen men doing it, and I don't know the origins of why it has become a pastime on the streets, but every Sunday morning you are sure to find a small group, or a handful of individuals, armed with what appear to be pretty vicious looking whips. Some of them seem really long and appear to have metal components woven into the structure, particularly around the handle area, in an attempt to kind of super charge their weapon. So what are these guys doing? Well it all seems to be about the 'crack'. The first thing that attracts you to the sight of this bunch of guys flailing around in a quiet corner of a public park is of course the noise. You are strolling round peacefully enjoying the Sunday morning ambience when suddenly there is this enormous supersonic crack nearby that shocks you out of your relaxation. And naturally you have to go and look for the source of this noise. I have seen this pastime in several cities now around the country, so I know it can't just be a regional thing. But of course, for someone to be flailing around cracking a whip, they need quite a lot of space, and the general public, not surprisingly, certainly seem to give these guys a very wide berth. So ultimately there are never more than 4 or 5 of these whip-crackers in any one group, as there isn't usually enough free open space to accommodate anymore, given all the thousands of people hanging around a public park at the weekend in China. I'm not really sure what you can do with a whip other than try and make the loudest crack possible, and to my untrained eye and ear, this seems to be the sole purpose of what these guys are aiming for. I kind of expected to see some fancy tricks, like I've seen on the TV with cowboys in rodeos in the US, but so far, I've never seen this kind of thing get incorporated into the Chinese public parkers. From my perspective as an uninitiated outsider, it seems a little simple and I imagine it would probably lose its appeal after the first few cracks, but these guys seem to take it very seriously. Whilst a few are practising in street clothes, it is normal for these guys to be dressed in elaborate robes, much like a kung fu master. This is just another example of how life on the street in China is just so different to other parts of the world. Imagine if someone took a massive, pimped up whip into a public park in the US or in Europe. They would be arrested in minutes for possession of a deadly weapon. China has such a different attitude to things. I'm not sure if the whip-crackers get to show off their skills at other venues, I've never seen it anywhere else. I can't imagine they would go down well at a children's party, but then again, this is China, so what do I know?

On deeper enquiry, I discovered that the whip-cracking thing is actually a very traditional form of Chinese pastime, so they are definitely not trying to copy US cowboys, maybe it's the other way around. Another equally unique but age-old tradition that you see in Chinese parks is the spinning tops. These are huge wooden cylinders with a sharp tip at the base that people (again usually men), try to keep up and spinning as long as possible. For this they also use a whip, but a kind of smaller, weedier version compared to the serious whip-crackers. I have actually seen less of this very traditional activity in my travels than the whip-crackers, so I assume it is slowly dying out as a pastime.

Another thing you will see in every public park and along many public leisure paths and coastal paths, is little outdoor exercise parks. We have these increasingly in Western countries, but in China they just seem to me to be more prevalent and more utilised. It is pretty common to see Chinese people hanging off one or other of the devices for stretching or some such exercise, yet in the West, whenever I see these public exercise parks, there is rarely anyone using them. People in the West seem somehow more self-conscious and don't like people staring at them when they are doing this kind of thing. But in China, people don't seem to suffer from such hang ups. There also seems to be more of a culture of exercise throughout the generations as well. It is usually older people who are on these devices, stretching their legs up in the air at angles impossible for your average Westerner let alone a Westerner from an older generation. It is really admirable and humbling to see.

By contrast, jogging appears less common in China compared to the West. It is quite unusual to see Chinese people out running in Chinese cities. My personal take on this is that it has something to do with all the traffic and pollution. I certainly never once went jogging out in the city for exactly these reasons. In a bigger city like Shanghai or Beijing, if you see someone out running, it is usually a foreigner. Although I do recall once seeing one Chinese lady jogging in a park in Shanghai. She was memorable because she was actually attempting to jog backwards. I understand it has some conditioning benefits, but it's still pretty weird and unusual seeing someone running backwards in public and I'm not sure I could bring myself to try it.

I always loved going to the public parks at the weekends. They are such a focal point for the local communities, and are always teeming with life and with a really great vibe to them. They are the best place for people watching and for experiencing a side of the Chinese lifestyle that you would otherwise never see. There is so much going on, so much to see, so much to photograph. Group dancing is not just confined to the public squares in the evening, you also see it going on at most public parks in the day at the weekends. There are a wide variety of dancing styles to watch, one of the most popular is classic ballroom dancing, and there is also usually a form of Chinese line dancing going on.

You will also usually find one or more people set up with microphones and loudspeakers in a kind of outdoor karaoke around a park. But this is definitely not karaoke. No one is singing Beyoncé. This is purely for middle aged crooners to sing traditional old Chinese songs. You know the kind, the ones that sound to us Westerners like nails being scrapped down a blackboard. Maybe this type of music is like alcohol, an acquired taste. But after over 6 years in China I am personally yet to acquire it. To me, hearing some old Chinese warbler screeching into a microphone in that high pitched nasally grating cacophony still feels like having a rat inside my head clawing at my ears to get out. A deeply and utterly unpleasant sensation. I know they take it seriously, but this is something that is just never going to be a cross-over to the West.

Other, more palatable, activities you regularly see in a Chinese park at the weekend include small groups of people playing Keepy Uppy using a weighted shuttlecock. This game is called JianZi and is a traditional national sport, not just a Sunday morning pastime. Somewhere in the park there will always be an area set aside for board games and the playing of cards. Every weekend you will inevitably see large groups of men massed around the tables playing a variety of games, including the very popular Chinese Chess (XianQi), which looks a bit like a cross between chequers and mahjong, but plays more like Western Chess. This game also spills out far beyond the park at weekends, and you will see it played on street corners, on the side of the road and in public squares throughout any city, again with groups of men huddled together. You may also get to see them playing the ubiquitous mahjong or a variety of card games. But whatever they are playing these games normally end up getting quite heated and vocal as spectators egg on the players.

A real treat to be found in public parks and spaces is the art of pavement calligraphy. This one was quite a surprise when I first saw it. We are all familiar with the beauty and traditions involved in writing Chinese characters, but normally you see this with brush on paper. When you hit the streets and parks of China, instead you will see people doing the same thing but armed with a really big brush, a pot of water and the pavement as their canvas. They 'paint' Chinese characters 20-30cm high on the concrete using only water as their medium. This seemed a bit incongruent when I first saw it as it is by definition a transient pastime. Whatever the person writes will disappear in a few minutes once the water evaporates away. I guess it's a great way to develop and show off their skills to the general public without the cost of materials and without building up a big portfolio to lug around. It is certainly fun to stand and watch these people at work. I guess the nearest equivalent in the West would be when you see chalk artists creating elaborate pictures on the floor in your local high street. Although the water characters they paint will evaporate quickly, one thing I have never yet seen is any of them stop and take a photo on their phone. This would seem the obvious way of capturing their artwork. Maybe they do and I just haven't been there at the right time, or maybe it is poor calligrapher's etiquette?

Another famous pastime associated with China is kite flying, and you will often see this in public parks, but due to the density of people at the weekend, kite flyers are more often to be found in large public squares or other wide open spaces. Some people take their kite flying very seriously. I have seen some very weird and wonderful kite designs over the years, some extreme mega-kites and some people flying their kites at seemingly impossible altitudes. I was lucky enough to visit the World Kite Museum in Weifang, Shandong province. I was there purely for business, and during an evening stroll I happened to notice this huge elaborately coloured building across the way. It was the museum. Who knew that Weifang, a city I had never heard of, was the official kite capital of the world? That really is the joy of travel, turning up somewhere you have never heard of and discovering something new and astounding. Weifang also hosts a major kite festival every year in April.

And parks are not just used for fun and exercise, they can serve as community service spaces as well. One Saturday morning as I wandered through Láodòng Gōngyuán (Labour Park), the big city park in the middle of Dalian, I found one corner crowded with a mix of old and young. On the grass verges all around there were paper notices, usually handwritten, with people were wandering around reading them. This struck me as pretty unusual, what could they be doing? I thought maybe this was some low tech, pre-digital version of eBay, with people advertising items or services for sale, but as I wandered round trying to read a few of the notices (this was about one year into my Chinese language lessons, so I was still quite rusty), I discovered that these were indeed adverts, just not for what I had expected, These were lonely hearts messages from old folk, looking for companionship. I could read the ages on a number of the posters, usually people in their 70's and 80's, and judging by the notices, exclusively widow(er)s who had lost their spouse. And the young people there seemed to be the families of the old folk. The younger people seemed to be doing most of the talking, and creating quite a buzz of chatter. I couldn't follow most of what they were saying at that stage, but it seemed to me that they were brokering matchmaking deals for their (grand)-parents. How sweet. What a great occasion and really admirable how their family were actively involved in helping their elders. Shows another big difference between the West and the East.

Another major pastime that can be seen in the public parks every weekend is Tai Chi and other forms of martial arts. Watching the slow, graceful movements of Tai Chi practitioners can be a relaxing experience both for the observer and certainly for the martial artist themselves. These guys are usually dressed up in all the traditional gear and it's a real cultural treat to get to see real people practicing real martial arts on the streets of China. Usually it's just a small group of 3 or 4, but sometimes just a single individual. These people are certainly not shy in demonstrating and practising their skills in public. Whilst I have seen some of the more aggressive combat martial arts styles on display in public parks, including styles of wushu and the occasional sword wielding guy, I personally don't see it that often as publically as I do Tai Chi. I guess the combat styles are generally practised behind closed doors in martial arts schools and normally only appear in public for displays. Watching people trying to beat each other up is probably not much of a crowd pleaser on a Sunday morning as part of your morning stroll, that's definitely more of a Saturday night after a few beers kind of crowd puller. The sword stuff is normally toned down anyway for safety, as they use wobbly, non-lethal replicas, and I'm guessing that carrying real swords around in public is probably banned, even in China. I actually saw much more real Kung Fu skills in action in another public park one Sunday morning, 18,500 km away from China, in

Ibirapuera Park in Sao Paulo. But that is another story for another book.

Martial arts is a real personal passion for me. I studied Kung Fu for 17 years back in the UK and attained black belt and instructor status, with a license to teach. So any trip to China, the birth place of Kung Fu, was always going to have a bit of a special feeling for me. My style was Hok Koon (crane fist) Kung Fu. Like many people my age, I grew up being spoon fed an ever increasing dose of martial arts movies on screen and TV as the genre grew in popularity. And was always admiring of the amazing things these guys could do. Who wouldn't want to be able to emulate them? But I was also a realist and as a kid not much of a sports person, preferring to have my head in a book rather than in someone's face. I knew it would take a lot of commitment and no doubt a lot of pain to become proficient in martial arts. That certainly wasn't for me. So I followed the scholarly path and studied hard, went to University, got a job, built a career and a family. Putting all my energies into these things. What changed for me was when my first marriage broke up in my late twenties. I suddenly found myself with no family, no money and lots of spare time on my hands. But what I did have was lots of pent up anger and frustration inside of me. I needed something new in my life. Fortunately I had a friend who was a student in a local Kung Fu club. We had already been going to the gym together for several months, so I was already building up some physical prowess. Since Kung Fu was something I had always had a yearning to learn, everything suddenly came together for me. So I swallowed my nerves and let my friend take me for my first lesson. This changed my life forever.

After many, many gallons of sweat and many years of pain later, plus a few cracked ribs, a dislocated jaw and numerous torn tendons, the highlight of my Kung Fu career came almost exactly twenty years after that first lesson. There was no way I could have foreseen that fate would have taken me to start a new life in the birthplace of Kung Fu, but there I was none the less. I wrote in an earlier chapter about all the demands of the Chinese New Year company parties I had to run the gauntlet of each January/February. One of the particular joys of the Chinese New Year company party that I didn't mention earlier, is that it is always highly participative. There is always a stage show, put on by the staff themselves, and as a boss in the company, you are absolutely expected to participate. This is another big 'out of your comfort zone' challenge for most Westerners. Professional business people are not normally the kind of people who like to get up on stage and entertain people, so the prospect of having to sing or dance in front of your work force can raise real fear in the most powerful of CEOs, and this for guys that regularly stand up in front of a tough business audience and give presentations. But this was a very different stage for them to tread. I know, I have been there, I have felt that fear, even though I actually have a bit of talent, since I can sing okay. I must admit, now that I have learnt to cope with all this, personally I enjoy seeing the discomfort in colleagues' eyes and in their body language when they have to get up and do their turn, it brings out the sadist in me.

The whole Chinese New Year stage show thing was yet another life enhancing, skill teaching experience for me. Thanks to the wonders of karaoke that I had been exposed to early on in my China life, by the time my first Chinese New Year party came along, I was okay with getting up and signing a karaoke song in front of an audience. But after 2 or 3 years of doing this I did feel I was taking the easy way out. After watching all of the dance choreography, sketches and other elaborate forms of entertainment that the staff and workers would put on, my karaoke song seemed a bit of a cop out, a bit of an easy fall back and a bit lame by comparison. I was looking for something else to do for future parties, something that would stand out and look like I had put some effort and preparation in, as a show of respect for the people. But such these things take preparation and practice of course. After all, no one wants to look a tit on stage. So what was I going to do different? Well one of my colleagues suggested to me, 'why don't you show us some Kung Fu? You've told us about your Kung Fu training many times over the years, let's see you actually do it for once'. What a great idea I thought.

At that point I admit my Kung Fu was getting a little rusty. I had asked myself every year during my 40s, do I really want to carry this on? As I got older I was starting to experience the inevitable, that your body starts to get brittle, more fragile and healing took so much longer than in my youth. But every year I continued because I loved it and just put up with the pain. I eventually threw in the towel on regular Kung Fu training when I moved to China. It was just such good timing for me. I had been training regularly for 17 years and moving to China meant I would have to find a new club and start again in another location. It just seemed like the right decision for me.

My Chinese New Year party Kung Fu stage debut came about 3 years after I had stopped regular training. I had kept my hand in, occasionally running through some simple set work in the gym, but nothing to the level I was doing before. So when I decided I was going to do a Kung Fu demonstration in front of my colleagues, it was back to the training ground for several weeks to dust off the cobwebs and unstiffen my joints. I had to build up a routine for a 10 minute display, which meant getting my old Kung Fu training notes out and trying to remind myself of some of the set patterns and deciding on some simple, but safe, combat techniques to demonstrate on an unsuspecting audience. I didn't want anyone ending up in the hospital after all. I was particularly wary of the event because as I have said before, these New Year events are always pretty boozy affairs. And I am well aware that, unlike vodka and tonic, alcohol and controlled Martials Arts environments do not mix. The decision to go with a Kung Fu demonstration as the only Westerner up on stage, proclaiming to show off Chinese Martial Arts skills to a room full of Chinese, always had the potential to kick off into a mass, Mao-tai fuelled brawl if I mistimed a kick and took some poor guy down. That would not have been good for my career.

Anyway, I practiced diligently, got myself back to a good enough standard and was ready for the big night. I had two opportunities to do my party piece. My company had two different factories in Shanghai, so we had two separate annual parties. One on Friday evening and the other on Saturday lunch time. In total I got to perform my display in front of around a thousand Chinese in all. I made sure I went up on stage early, and no drinking beforehand, so I could stay in total control during my demo. It all went very well, I dragged a few audience members up on stage for some 'one on one' action, no one got hurt and there was no mass brawl. A very special occasion for me, and I felt a real sense of achievement for standing up and stepping up to the plate.

When moving to China, I mentioned that I decided to hang up my Kung Fu sash at that point and retire. But apart from the martial arts skilled I learnt, there was another aspect of 17 years of learning Kung Fu that I thought would stand me in good stead with my move and that is the language. As part of our studies in the style, all instructions in our lessons would be in Chinese, so I learnt many basic Chinese words, like simple numbers, and simple instructions, or so I thought. I was told for 17 years that what I was taught was Chinese, but guess what I found when I actually moved to China and started learning Chinese? The words I had been taught were not Chinese at all, they were Cantonese. It was obvious in hindsight because our Kung Fu style had originated in Hong Kong, so it wasn't surprising that the instructions had been built up in the Cantonese language. So it turned out that my 17 years of learning had done absolutely zero towards giving me a grounding in the Chinese language, which is Mandarin, not Cantonese. So I really was starting again from scratch.

Just like everywhere else in the world, there has been a big growth in gym culture around China in recent years, and new gyms appear to pop up frequently in every city. Another result of a growing middle class with disposable income, a broader appreciation of healthy living and ever increasing overseas influence. As a sub-culture of the gym trend, body building is also becoming popular. I remember one occasion during our first year in Dalian, we were walking through a local shopping mall and they were holding a men's body building contest. Quite strange as a Westerner to see all these distorted Chinese guys, covered in fake tan. I have a fantastic photo of Julie standing next to one of the guys. He's so dark he really looks like he's been dipped in chocolate.

Above all sports, Dalian is associated in China with football. One of its nicknames is the 'football city'. Driving around the city centre, you cannot miss the huge statue of a football sitting at the top of a hill as the centrepiece of Labour Park. Dalian has two professional football clubs,

Dalian Yifang and Dalian Transcendence. Yifang is the bigger of the two clubs, playing in the top flight Chinese Super League, whilst Transcendence plays in the league below, China League One. Yifang plays its home matches at the Dalian Sports Centre Stadium, a massive modern arena which is part of an Olympic sized sports site, with world class swimming, tennis, basketball and baseball facilities, amongst others. Transcendence plays out of the older Jinzhou Stadium. Dalian clubs have a strong history of top level football, with Dalian's former club, Dalian Wanda, later renamed to Dalian Shide, having won the Chinese Super League eight times, and still considered one of the most successful clubs in Chinese football history. The club closed in 2012 due to financial difficulties and match fixing scandals. As an outsider looking in, many football teams in China seem to regularly change their names, reflecting changes in ownership, and seem to drift in and out of business due to financial mishandling and scandals. This must make it quite difficult for teams to retain any loyal fan base. The Chinese Super League has sixteen teams, with Guangzhou Evergrande usually the top team and certainly the most well-known of the sixteen internationally, thanks to its high profile signings of international coaches and players in recent years.

Football is surprisingly popular amongst young Chinese and there is much talk about football socially, just like back in Britain. The standard of Chinese football itself still lags far behind the level required to be taken seriously on the world stage, and as with many other areas in China, there is much investment going in to try to change that. But it takes time to develop grass roots talent that will make a difference to the national team. Just as in other areas of business, football attracts expats, due to the amount of money washing around. Famous coaches and players find their way to China towards the end of their careers lured by big money. Teams in the Super League are allowed a maximum of four foreigners per squad. One foreign coach I met entertained me with great tales about how he and his team got paid big cash bonuses. The whole team would have to line up in the car park after a match, with him at the front, and the owner would hand out each person's cut from a huge pile of cash in a plastic bag out of the back of his car.

We were lucky enough to make friends with a handful of expat players and staff at both Dalian teams, who would regularly treat us to free tickets for games in their VIP box. Our driver Mr Fang loved this, as he was a big football fan, so when we started giving the Transcendence number one striker, Ivan Božić, a lift to the games, he couldn't believe it. Ivan was from Sarajevo in Bosnia-Herzegovina and had played for their national team. We got to know him because he lived at the Shangri-La with us. Ivan was very popular with the fans and our car would get stopped regularly by fans when leaving the stadium after a game to get his autograph and a few selfies. Ivan was always happy to get support from his Shangri-La neighbours, and so was really pleased when Julie organised a big coach load of friends from the Shangri-La to attend the big local derby between the two Dalian teams.

Ivan and I shared a love of tennis and so we started to play regularly together on the Shangri-La courts. As he was 18 years my junior, and a professional sportsman, I was pretty pleased with myself that I could keep up with him. He was a very good tennis player and definitely taught me a few things, so it was great for my game. In passing one day he happened to mention that he used to play so much tennis that he almost became a professional tennis player instead of a footballer, and that his playing partner was

Marin Čilić. If you don't know your tennis, Marin Čilić won a Grand Slam title at the 2014 US Open and was ranked as the world number 3 early in 2018. The year I was playing a lot of tennis with Ivan, 2017, Čilić even got into the Wimbledon final against Roger Federer. Blimey, no wonder Ivan was so good! We still keep in touch via WeChat and Ivan is still a close friend of Čilić, attending his wedding in 2018.

I mentioned earlier that one of my big passions was Kung Fu, but that middle age and too many injuries made me decide to give it up when we moved to China. So I had to look for another sporting pastime that I could replace the void in my life with. I had always fancied taking up tennis. All that running around and ball skills appealed to me and it was a one on one combative type of sport, just like martial arts, but without the full contact of the fighting arts, so seemed to tick all the boxes for me. Plus, the Shangri-La had two tennis courts on site, one indoor and one outdoor. So Julie and I started playing tennis together regularly. Julie was a much better player than me. Being ambidextrous probably helped, especially when she could just switch hands to play a shot, which is very disconcerting when you're always on the receiving end of forehands, whichever side of the court you play the ball. We played a lot of tennis in the first couple of years, and started playing doubles with some other couples, one French and the other Spanish. I had transferred from Kung Fu to tennis to reduce the impact on my body, but we were playing so much tennis at one point that Julie and I both ended up with knee problems. All that twisting and rapid change of direction takes its toll. So we both had to stop playing and get treatment. It took 18 months to fully recover and that taught us a valuable lesson about just how much tennis we should be playing to avoid knee strain.

Tennis has also grown in popularity in China, due to the success of the women's tennis player Li Na, who won the French and Australian Open titles. We would regularly go down to Shanghai to see the annual men's Shanghai Masters tournament every October, which attracted all the big names every year. The stadium there is fantastic, but quite a long way out of the city. Dalian also hosts an annual women's international tennis event, which is fun to watch.

EPILOGUE

I feel privileged to have lived in China through some of the most important years in China's modern history. Julie & I have been so lucky to see first-hand many of the dramatic changes sweeping across the country and its society, at a pace you just don't see in Western countries. But despite this opening up of the country and all its modernisation and digitisation, in many ways, China is still like the Wild West, opening up new frontiers all the time, and still a land of opportunity. And our expat experience opened up not just China, but the whole world for us, because it gave us so many friends in so many places.

As in many cultures, the etiquette and traditional customs of behaviour are slowly drifting as new generations come along. Even in our 6 years in China we saw the country changing. Such changes have been lead from two ends of the spectrum.

Firstly by the government, who launched a big anti-corruption drive (or anti-graft as they call it). This began with some very high profile cases with top officials, which over time, cascaded down the ranks into a serious hunt for corruption at all official levels. To be fair, government spending and skimming had got seriously out of hand at the provincial level, and the tales of senior officials being caught with $100m's in gold hidden in their house were just incredible and not one-offs. You just had to see one of their official dinners to understand how cash was being splashed around. They became infamous as ultra-decadent affairs, which directly caused a massive spike in Maotai prices as officials sort to outdo each other by putting on the most lavish spreads with the most expensive bái jiǔ's on the table. The clampdown on such frivolous spending has had a far reaching effect on restaurants and hotels, as the lucrative trade in hosting such events virtually disappeared overnight, and on the prices of Maotai, which have dropped to more sensible and sustainable levels.

I went to China for business, and as part of doing business there, inevitably the whole subject of bribery and corruption reared its head a number of times, but what really constitutes corruption? When you look back far enough, every civilised society around the world has built their economies on corruption and slave labour. It's just that when an economy grows to a sufficient scale and infrastructure, the country decides to grow a conscience and start imposing rules and ethics. So it's difficult to judge China against that backdrop. They are just still in that earlier stage of economic regulation. They will get there, but it will just take more time. Patience is required.

As a Westerner, it is hard to appreciate that Chinese people live in a society where they do not vote, and have no democracy. It seems like an alien concept to us in many Western countries. I am not a particularly political person, and I do not mean to judge, but from my point of view there appear to be good and bad things about each of the political systems. But what I do see is that the Chinese have achieved so much and continue to do so. China appears to have transformed itself into the biggest Capitalist state on the planet, yet politically it is a Communist state. Maybe they are moving towards the best of both ideologies?

The second wave of change that is transforming modern China, has been the emergence of a new generation of young people, with new attitudes and new expectations. Much has been written about the Chinese one child policy and about the unforeseen effects of population control. My direct experience is of working with a new breed of Chinese youngsters who grew up as only children, doted on by their parents and growing up during a time when the Chinese economy was growing up massively around them. They have grown up on daily stories in the newspaper and on TV of all these mega-wealthy Chinese entrepreneurs, like Jack Ma of Ali Baba and Wang Jianlin of the Wanda Group. And they have become a generation of young adults that just expect things to be handed to them on a plate. They are used to having everything they wanted from their parents, and they expect to become the next mega-rich entrepreneur, because that's what people do in China, don't they? They have also grown up in a time when China has been opening up massively to the West, with all the influences and opportunities that offers. And in a time when China has embraced and taken control of the digital age. China now has a generation of well educated, English speaking, intelligent young adults with attitude. They are changing the country, they are changing the culture and they are hungry for more.

After over 6 years living in China, I definitely became institutionalised. To the point that going back to the UK became a strange and uncomfortable experience for me. I found the British customs, ways of doing things and their attitudes quite alien and difficult for me to relate to. Not to mention the terrible food and weather. Every day I was back in the UK, it always seemed a dull, grey, overcast, drizzly event. When I was growing up this was just normal. It was only when I moved somewhere that wasn't like this every day that I began to appreciate what an effect the weather has on people's moods. A bright sunny day definitely makes for a bright sunny disposition. And the food was always so stodgy when I went back to the UK, chips with everything. Like Britain was stuck in a great big gungy mess of starch and sugar, Carbohydrate City. Eating back in Britain became a very tough experience for me, making me lethargic, and making it increasingly difficult to lift up my fork to grab another chip.

As I have grown older, slowly inching towards, but never entirely reaching maturity, life has demonstrated to me many times that you only gain more from it by stepping out of your comfort zone, by trying and doing new things, taking yourself beyond what you know and what you think you are capable of. This was exactly the reason I moved to China. China has taught me so much. China has transformed me as a person and has absolutely shaped how I choose to live the rest of my life.

Thank you for reading,

Andy Wynn

CONCLUSION

So that's it, that's our story. We hope you enjoyed this quick jaunt through our time living in China. We have tried to include all the most important, educational and entertaining facts, stories and incidents, but there are many more stories we have left to share.

We said at the start, that we were motivated to write this book to help educate people in the West about China and to dispel the misinformed attitudes that many still have. So, we hope we've given you a flavour of what to expect when you travel to China and opened your mind to the richness of culture that awaits you.

One sad fact we observed is that too many foreigners live and work in China and just stay within their expat community the whole time. Why? Because it's the easy option. We had friends whose whole life revolves around their work. Their friends are foreign work friends, their social life is just going to an endless stream of expat parties with the same group of foreigners. They have no Chinese friends, they have never taken the time to get to know local people. Don't get me wrong, the whole expat social scene is great fun, but always staying within that circle will always keep you on the outside of China looking in. Until you befriend real local Chinese people, and spend time with them in their social settings, you can never truly experience and learn about the culture, about the different approaches to life that the China experience offers you. You will be missing out on a huge chunk of your China experience if you do not step out of your expat comfort zone.

It was hard moving to China, at times it was certainly tough living there, but absolutely the hardest thing of all was when we finally had to leave China. As an expat, you are reliant on your local employment contract to get your work visa, so that you can stay in the country, and once you have completed your contract, your time is up and you have to go back home, or on to another assignment, so it is always going to be a finite deal. Although plenty of single expat guys end up staying permanently by marrying Chinese girls, giving them residency rights. For us, we went for 3 years, but managed to extend the work contract for another 3 years, so we feel we did exceptionally well hanging on by our finger nails as long as we could. When you know the end is in sight, you do the inevitable stuff like making a list of all the places you hadn't been yet and trying to fit them all in before you go home. Our departure was such a sad day. We had seen so many of our friends come and go, and had stood in their farewell party so many times, and each time we knew that one day it would be our farewell and it would be us stepping out of the doors of the Shangri-La for the final time. It is very difficult to say goodbye to so many friends that you have become so close to.

We also explained at the start of this book how living in Dalian exposed us to such a wide circle of international expat friends from so many different countries, including Spain, Norway, Brazil, Columbia, Korea, Japan, Malaysia,

China, Philippines, France, Germany, Finland, Sweden, Australia, USA, and many other countries. Many of these people have since returned to their home countries, but thanks to the wonders of social media we all stay in regular contact, but usually through WeChat, something not used in most of our host countries, so it's like having your own personal social media platform. But more than that, it's like having your own personal Air BnB network as well, because it gives us all such a great excuse to travel round the world visiting our good friends, in places where you always know you'll have a bed for the night. It truly is a privilege to see all these wonderful people again as we continue to travel, and keep our friendships and our shared experiences alive.

During our six years in Dalian, our friends were our family, and Dalian, for so many years was, and in some ways will always be, our home.

Andy & Julie Wynn

ACKNOWLEDGEMENTS

None of this would have been possible without all the great friends and colleagues that made our time in China so special.

We would like to extend our heartfelt thanks to so many people;

To Ian Robb for sending us there in the first place.

To our DMC work colleagues and good friends; Matt, Gong, Jacky, Snow.

To our amazing drivers; Huang and Fang.

To all the friends that kept us sane over the years; Frank, Dominic, Rabiab, Dorian, William, Ning, Tina, Mike & Sue, Craig & Ronnie, David & Julie, Ken & Lyn, Mikael & Jessica, Martin & Galina, Peter & Yujia, Sheila & Danny, David & Desiree.

To all the Staff and friends of the Shangri-La; Martin, Nancy, Mika, Beata, Wendy, Amber, Rainie, Apple, Coco, Sunny, David and all the other wonderful staff past and present too numerous to mention.

To all the Shangri-La entertainers; Waldo, Maria, Slice, Helen, Yulka and Cindy.

To Andy's tennis coach Helen, and to Philippe & Claire,

and Isabel & Fernando, for many hours of fun on the tennis court.

To Leon & Serena for all the delicious food at Leon's.

To Moritz, Jim and the Grand Hyatt staff for some very special evenings.

To Ivan & Antonia, David & Alina for all our football fun and VIP football tickets.

To Isabelle & Raphael, Priscilla, Anna, Anara, Marcia and to all of our Brazilian friends.

To Julie's fantastic Zumba teacher Brie for hours of fun keeping fit and to all her workout buddies, Nancy, Angellu & family, Yushiko, Kaori, Madori, Megan, Kimberly & Vanessa.

To all of the wonderful wives who participated and enjoyed Julie's 'Shangri-La bubble' chat, to all the 'Dalian hotties' chat members and also special thanks to the members of Julie's 'Worldwide hotties' group chat.

To all Julie's Mahjong group players; Sharmila, Megumi, Fumiko, Chihiro, Lyn, Theresa, Vivianne, Ivy, Phoebe, Takako, Beula, Joanne, Sonja, Jennifer, Sachiko, Isabel, Izi, Karen, Tjais, Sandy, Michelle, Amercie, Flavia, Etsuko, Sedef, Watarai, Trish, Soojung, Sujin, Antoinette, and special thanks to Tony & Annie and all the staff at Cafe Copenhagen for hosting so many of the games and for all the delicious food, birthday cake and many other special occasion surprises, also thanks to Linlin for her art classes and inspiration.

Julie would also like to send a special thank you to her Dalian hairdresser Sebastian and his amazing assistant Snow, and to all at Kelly's salon and her nail girls.

And finally, to our amazing Chinese teacher, Summer.

We will never forget you all.

ABOUT THE AUTHOR

Dr Andy Wynn has spent over 30 years in industry, working all over the world in industrial manufacturing businesses. He is an international business leader and former CTO at a billion dollar multinational.

His career long passion has been creating new technologies and building new businesses from them and is the author of a leading book on the subject of innovation and new product development, 'Transforming Technology into Profit', and the founder of TTIP Consulting Ltd, an international consulting firm that helps industrial businesses grow by accelerating their delivery of better, more profitable new products. More information can be found at www.ttipconsulting.co.uk.

A seasoned world traveller and global citizen, Andy's career has taken him all over the world, working in North and South America, throughout Europe, the Middle East and right across Asia and Australia. He has a particular passion for China, having spent 20 years regularly travelling and doing business there, including over 6 years living there.

Andy is a regular speaker at conferences and business

schools on the subjects of 'Unlocking Innovation in Business' and 'Doing Business in China' and regularly speaks on industry trends.

In his spare time, Andy is very active and spends much of his free time in the gym or outdoors. He spent 17 years studying Kung Fu and has a black belt and is a licensed instructor. As middle age and injuries began to take their toll, he swapped Kung Fu for tennis and has been playing regularly for several years now.

He is an accomplished musician and singer and has been playing electric guitar since he was 16. His album 'Never Too Late' was released on Office Records in 2012, and is available on iTunes and many other digital media outlets.

Andy now lives in Marbella, Spain with his wife Julie.